SIMPLY STRATEGY

Prentice Hall
FINANCIAL TIMES

In an increasingly competitive world, we believe it's quality of thinking that gives you the edge – an idea that opens new doors, a technique that solves a problem, or an insight that simply makes sense of it all. The more you know, the smarter and faster you can go.

That's why we work with the best minds in business and finance to bring cutting-edge thinking and best learning practice to a global market.

Under a range of leading imprints, including *Financial Times Prentice Hall*, we create world-class print publications and electronic products bringing our readers knowledge, skills and understanding, which can be applied whether studying or at work.

To find out more about Pearson Education publications, or tell us about the books you'd like to find, you can visit us at **www.pearsoned.co.uk**

PEARSON
Education

SIMPLY

STRATEGY

The shortest route to the best strategy

Richard Koch and Peter Nieuwenhuizen

FT Prentice Hall
FINANCIAL TIMES

An imprint of **Pearson Education**

Harlow, England • London • New York • Boston • San Francisco • Toronto
Sydney • Tokyo • Singapore • Hong Kong • Seoul • Taipei • New Delhi
Cape Town • Madrid • Mexico City • Amsterdam • Munich • Paris • Milan

PEARSON EDUCATION LIMITED

Edinburgh Gate
Harlow CM20 2JE
Tel: +44 (0)1279 623623
Fax: +44 (0)1279 431059
Website: www.pearsoned.co.uk

First published in Great Britain in 2006

ISBN-13: 978-0-273-70878-0
ISBN-10: 0-273-70878-3

British Library Cataloguing in Publication Data
A catalogue record for this book is available from the British Library

Library of Congress Cataloging-in-Publication Data
A catalog record for this book is available from the Library of Congress

10 9 8 7 6 5 4 3 2 1
10 09 08 07 06

Typeset by 30
Printed and bound in Great Britain by Bell & Bain Ltd, Glasgow

The Publisher's policy is to use paper manufactured from sustainable forests.

DISCLAIMER

Pearson Education would like to make clear that it is not the owner of the software entitled Simply Strategy referred to in this book and is in no way responsible for its provision. We can offer no customer support nor can this product be bought through Pearson Education. We can make no guarantee as to the availability of the software at any point in time. For information please refer to *www.simplystrategy.com*

CONTENTS

This book is dedicated to Phil Cooke, and to Lubertus Nieuwenhuizen (1918–2005), for his kindness and uncompromising faith in our good intentions

FOREWORD

We penned this book to strip away the mysteries from strategy and explain in plain language how a successful business strategy can be developed. We write for practical managers – those running business units or divisions, and entrepreneurs. We've spent much of our lives helping operating managers develop great strategy that raises profits and growth. In doing this we've often wanted simple and cheap reference materials – a good book or a software program. We couldn't find them. So we've provided them ourselves. A powerful method, yet common sense and designed for practical people. But also rooted in numbers to raise the bottom line. The approach here can liberate executives – developing a profitable strategy can be easy and fun as well as hugely rewarding.

Far more is known about strategy than five or ten or twenty years ago, yet never has strategy seemed more baffling to the practical manager. Knowledge has not bred clarity. A profusion of (mostly well-intended) tools, terms and techniques has caused bewilderment, instead of promoting the very real value of strategy to those who need it most. Result? For many managers, strategy has come to seem meaningless, difficult, hopelessly academic.

But don't despair. Once you strip away from strategy its dazzling and distracting garments, and reveal the raw, naked power underneath, the basic concepts are clear, accessible, powerful, practical, highly useful and relatively uncontroversial. For us, strategy is the super-hero of the past 50 years of commercial experience – its value has been justified by logic, intuition, experience and practice alike. You'll come to see why as you read this book and apply its tools. We're confident that you'll share our faith in strategy, and profit from it.

BUSINESS UNIT STRATEGY – THE SUCCESS STORY

By far the greatest value of strategy is at the sharp end of business, where operating managers are fighting to create and deliver products and services that customers will like more than those from competing firms. Strategy is most useful when used by practical managers as they go about their daily activities, deciding how to deploy their time, insight, money and the talent of colleagues.

Business strategy is always very powerful when it is sensibly developed and used by operating managers. Few people realize this. Corporate strategy has hogged the limelight at the expense of business strategy. More than 80 per cent of strategy literature is about corporate strategy, for a small audience of chief executives and their staff. Worse still, business strategy has usually been developed by anyone but the people who should be developing it – the operating managers in the trenches. Instead, business strategy has typically been the province of the head office or consulting firms.

We aim to put that right and put line managers back in the driving seat.

HOW TO USE THIS BOOK

Part One sets the scene, providing a short introduction and explaining where corporate and business unit strategy differ and overlap.

Part Two is the heart of the book – a step-by-step, do-it-yourself guide to business unit strategy. There are two extended cases to illustrate how the method can work for your business. We show how Richard worked with the chief executive of United Tea Company to quickly come up with a top-down strategy. By contrast, Peter tells the story of his work in building a "bottom-up" global strategy for Addit Ltd, with heavy involvement of managers throughout the firm. We see how a company can focus on its best activities and market positions to increase profitability, while energizing its employees and creating a shared understanding of future direction.

Part Three explains how to realize your strategy; how to make it work in practice.

Finally, we provide two Appendices. Appendix One takes you on a brisk trot through historical trends in strategic thinking. Appendix Two is an A–Z glossary of terms, comprising short and provocative essays on the strategic subjects mentioned in this book. It's best used as reference material, although it's also good company on plane journeys when you can dip into it at random for a quick read to make you think.

WHAT'S DIFFERENT AND BETTER ABOUT THIS BOOK?

◆ *Plain language and easy-to-use techniques*. *Proven methods already tested in both large and small organizations.*

◆ *Focus on how to make money*. *We show how to split your business up into chunks that show dramatically different profitability. Time after time executives are stunned at these results. Time after time we find that 20 per cent of sales result in 80 per cent or more of total profit.*

◆ *Do-it-yourself, fast and cost-effective. Business strategy is immensely rewarding. Given their experience and dedication, business managers and owners are in a unique position to develop their own strategies and improve their company's performance. With this book you can do so yourself, or rely on some very focused help. Whichever you choose, you will save a lot of money and time.*

Finally, although this book is written for operating managers and business owners, it may also be used by corporate executives to promote a consistent strategy across all their businesses. Our approach will not just benefit your managers and businesses, it will create a common language and generate company-wide improvements.

OUR SOFTWARE CAN HELP

We discovered that working through all the numbers when developing strategy can take a lot of time and get in the way of what you're trying to do. So, we have pioneered software that presents the important facts about your business in a snazzy way, as well as saving you lots of time. You can find out more about the package and buy it from our website *www.simplystrategy.com*.

LET US KNOW

We are passionate about the power of strategy and the value of our method. We've seen how it excites teams and transforms businesses, and multiplies their profits. That's why we wrote this book and the software.

But you are the judge of whether we have succeeded in our efforts. We'd like to hear about your experiences using our method. Please tell us what you think.

Reach us at contact@simplystrategy.com, or leave a message at *www. simplystrategy.com*. We look forward to hearing from you!

Richard Koch
Peter Nieuwenhuizen

AUTHORS' ACKNOWLEDGEMENTS

In previous books I've thanked very many people who've framed my view of strategy and I'd simply like to thank them again, en masse. They know who they are and trees are better alive. But I must single out, in recent years, Marcus Alexander, Eric Benedict, Andrew Campbell, Charles Coates, Ian Godden, Chris Outram, Peter Johnson, Martin Nye, and Jamie Reeve – if only because one or two of them might complain otherwise. I must also praise my assistants Aaron Calder and Douglas ('Dougal') Blowers, who are both wonderfully cheerful in the face of my many demands. And, however briefly, I must thank my dear friends who have made and make my daily life such a joy, especially Dominique, Juliet, Lee, Matthew, Patrick, Peter, Philip, and Robin. Finally, though I am usually rude about publishers, we've had a great experience with Liz Gooster, Laura Brundell and Richard Stagg, who have devoted unusual attention to this book and been efficient, pleasant and supportive throughout.

Richard Koch

Many people have contributed to the development of my thoughts and the resulting book material. I owe them all a great deal of appreciation. Special thanks are due to my colleagues at Akzo Nobel. I'm also grateful to Frederik van Oene of Arthur D. Little for his insight on core competencies and to Mario Jaeckel of Prochemics for his valuable input on competitor analysis.

Thanks particularly to Daniel Schroeder of Kendall Consulting and Ginny Reck who read the drafts, providing rapid and helpful feedback. Ginny also generously contributed her expertise on value disciplines. All this has been an enormous help.

Our collaboration with Boden on the software has been vital. A fast-growing, innovative IT provider, Boden's people have opened my eyes to the new and global domain of software development. Working simultaneously in New Jersey, various European locations, and Bangalore, India, we've enjoyed the late-night calls with Sashidhar Reddy and Kumar Margasahayam. Above all, we want to thank Babu Sampath and Rangarajan Kumar for the trust they put in our vision.

Personally, I'm deeply grateful to Christina for her love and support, unwavering and often across great distances. Thank you for teaching me new perspectives on life and even, just possibly, how to like cats.

Peter Nieuwenhuizen

PUBLISHER'S ACKNOWLEDGEMENTS

We are grateful to the following for permission to reproduce copyright material:

Illustration 15 is adapted with the permission of The Free Press, a Division of Simon & Schuster Adult Publishing Group, from COMPETITIVE STRATEGY: Techniques for analyzing industries and competitors by Michael E. Porter. Copyright © 1980, 1998 by The Free Press. All rights reserved.

In some instances we have been unable to trace the owners of copyright material, and we would appreciate any information that would enable us to do so.

PART ONE

INTRODUCTION

INTRODUCTION

THE JOY OF STRATEGY

Strategy is fun! Plotting the strategy for your own business may be the most rewarding and fulfilling thing you do this year. If you read this book – just Part Two will do if you are in a hurry – you will *enjoy* devising your strategy and your firm will make a lot more money. So should you!

(And if you buy our software, you'll be able to plug in all your numbers and, hey presto!, you'll have wonderful charts drawn summarizing what really matters for your business.)

The strategy of *individual* businesses is one of the most important forces in the universe. The force lies in the creation of wealth from raw materials that nobody else thought to use in that way. Because each business and each part of a business is different from any other business, it's possible to make a lot of money and have happy customers. The trick is to follow the rules of strategy – which are now proven, easy to understand, and easy to use – to create something different and better, so that particular sets of customers like your product more than any other and competitors can't copy you.

These simple rules of strategy have been made to sound complicated and forbidding by the experts – academics and consultants – who want you to depend on them. But the truth is that the rules of strategy are a lot less difficult to grasp than the rules of poker. And a lot more profitable too!

All you need is a simple guide that makes plotting strategy sound as easy as it really is. You're holding that guide in your hands.

BUT WHAT IS STRATEGY?

Most simply, strategy can be defined as the rules and actions used to steer a business towards making much more money.

Strategy comes in two flavor. There is *corporate* strategy – plotting the direction of a portfolio of businesses, usually by a corporate head office. That's important, but if you are a practical manager or an entrepreneur, that's not what you need. [1]

Then there is *business* strategy – crafting the strategy for individual businesses. That's what you need. That's what this book is about. [2]

A FRESH VIEW OF BUSINESS STRATEGY

Business strategy is strategy developed for individual, self-contained businesses, supplying one main market. These units can be part of larger corporations, or stand-alone small- or medium-sized businesses. Contrary to popular belief, the concepts of strategy are most valuable when used by managers running self-contained businesses. It's at the business level that managers have to decide where and how to spend their limited resources – their own time, the talents of their people and the cash entrusted to them. If you're a business owner or operational manager, business strategy can:

◆ *help you define the different parts of your business, where you need to do different things to be successful;*

◆ *show in detail where you make the most profits and cash, and why;*

◆ *understand the customer's perspective and why people buy from you or from competitors;*

◆ *indicate where you should concentrate most effort and cash;*

◆ *work out the extent of likely profit improvement opportunity, from changing product/customer mix, prices and/or cutting costs;*

◆ *help you to understand why you have been successful or unsuccessful in particular areas and initiatives;*

◆ *show up any missing skills;*

◆ *identify business segments or product lines that should be discontinued or sold;*

◆ *show which customers should be cultivated most and how to lock them into the firm's products for ever;*

---

[1] If you *are* interested in corporate strategy, if you are running a big group of businesses for example, then you've got the wrong book. The book you need is Richard Koch (2006, third edition) *The Financial Times Guide to Strategy*, FT Prentice Hall, London.

[2] Many people refer to 'business unit strategy'. We prefer 'business strategy' as it's simpler. But the terms mean exactly the same.

◆ *develop business culture and competencies so that it can be more successful than competitors at meeting the needs of its best customers.*

WHO SHOULD DEVELOP STRATEGY?

It's silly for one set of people to draw up a plan and then hand it over to another group of people to implement. Yet what's silly often happens. Outside strategists – consultants or people from head office – develop the plans, kick off the strategy, then retire to a safe distance, handing implementation to managers. Then the outsiders monitor the results and complain about them. That approach usually bombs. Neither the strategists nor the managers are to blame. The flaw lies in the process itself.

A strategy has to be adapted to real-life relationships between employees, customers, suppliers, and other people. Any strategic shift has to be gradually introduced, crafted and re-crafted. Some changes won't work at all and must be junked. Other changes have some of the desired effects but unexpected and unwelcome side-effects – these changes have to be modified. Yet other innovations work amazingly well and should be rolled out more vigorously and completely. Only managers can do this. A strategy will only work if the executives pursuing it understand it, believe in it, and have the authority and confidence to dump or develop different parts of the strategy in response to feedback.

Business strategy should be developed by operating managers in each strategic business unit (SBU) – in each self-contained business serving one main market.

Yet there can be a problem even with this approach. Major strategy revision rarely happens once a quarter or even once a year. Most businesses will do a 'strategy proper' every seven to ten years, and even the most assiduous would only review strategy every three to five years, with small tune-ups in between. As a result, most managers are unfamiliar with how to develop a strategy. Even if they are allowed to take on the task – which usually they are not – managers are understandably reluctant to do so.

So businesses often bring in strategy consultants. They develop a strategy and are actively involved in its implementation, gradually fading out (sometimes, very gradually) as the operating managers feel more and more comfortable with their control of the strategy and ability to adapt it.

The method is very expensive. Before a strategy advice can be formulated, the consultants have to acquire a thorough understanding of the business and its environment. The team of consultants has to be well rounded to cover all aspects of business operations, and high-caliber to comprehend these quickly. The team has to gather extensive information from within and outside of the business, and come to grips with it. Only then can it start to formulate and evaluate the various strategic options.

The high fees are warranted, the consultants say, by the profit improvement they can bring. What the consultants don't say, however, is that all of the benefits from their work, and more, could often be obtained if the operating managers developed the strategy themselves. Almost everyone assumes this is impossible. They are wrong.

Armed with the book you hold in your hands (and our software), you can devise your own strategy. The only help you might consider would be a 'strategy facilitator', someone with practical knowledge of developing strategy. The facilitator may be available inside the firm, or can be hired short-term from the outside. The facilitator works with the operating managers to develop the strategy, without taking over responsibility for making the decisions. Whether you use a facilitator or not, we'll show you how to craft your own strategy, and have fun doing so.

BUSINESS STRATEGY IN TEN EASY STEPS

Originality in strategic thinking is much less important than synthesizing what is available. One has to be clear where the different approaches are most useful and about the trade-offs between them. Most of all it's about putting the heart of strategy back where it belongs, at the sharp end of business unit reality. In our charter for business strategy this means two things:

◆ *placing emphasis on building strategy from the bottom up, based on numbers – the sales and particularly the profits made by the different activities;*

◆ *employing a synthesis of the 'positioning view' of strategy and of what is often seen as the competing 'resource-based view'. (Read more on this in Appendix One.)*

We're about to run through ten easy steps to develop business strategy.

Each step has been tested in large and small organizations and proven its value over many years and under many different circumstances. We promise that the ten steps will give you the most 'bang for your buck'.

ILLUSTRATION 1.1

Ten easy steps for plotting your strategy

Step	Title	Objective
1	What business are you in?	Segment your business according to your customers and your competition
2	Where do you make the money?	Define your true profitability by segment, by product and by customer
3	How good are your competitive positions?	Determine the strength of your positions
4	What skills and capabilities underpin your success?	Find out what you do well and why you are successful in your business
5	Is this a good market to be in?	Determine the attractiveness of your markets
6	What do the customers think?	Learn about the views of your customers and what that means for how you do business
7	What about the competitors?	Get insight into your competitors and their perspective on the business
8	Should you do something else?	Decide where to innovate in your business
9	Who are you, and what will you do?	Finalize your strategy by defining what you are now, who you want to be and how to change
10	How can you raise profits quickly?	Decide the steps to take for short-term improvements

It's now time to start – with a strategy for your own business ...

PART TWO

BUSINESS STRATEGY

1

OVERVIEW

Business strategy is the process of developing strategy for a single, largely self-contained business. The business unit could be a whole company if it is small or medium-sized (or even in a large company focused on a single line of business), or a separate, largely autonomous part of a larger company, comprising a profit centre that has its own set of external customers and competitors (often called an SBU, 'strategic business unit, or 'business unit', or 'business' – we will generally use one of the two latter terms).

This Part will take you through a step-by-step guide to develop strategy for your business. It assumes you have a real business for which you wish to develop or validate strategy. If you don't, it will be easier and more rewarding for you to think of a business you know fairly well – perhaps that of a friend or relative or one you have worked in – and imagine that you are developing its strategy.

The first thing to appreciate is that developing a strategy is not difficult. It is only made to seem difficult by the strategy 'professionals': academics, corporate planners and consultants. Anyone with a reasonable degree of intelligence and knowledge about business can develop a strategy. The first barrier to overcome is the sense of intimidation or fear of stepping over the threshold.

The second barrier is the jargon. The language of strategy is often peculiar. As with most fields of study, the jargon is useful as a form of shorthand once you have mastered it. We will try to explain exactly what we mean by any unfamiliar term, but if you run into difficulties, refer to the Glossary in Appendix Two. All terms listed in Appendix Two appear in the text in small capitals when used for the first time. A bit of patience and perseverance should soon make the meaning clear.

The third barrier is the compilation and presentation of the information about your business. This can be done by hand or with a spreadsheet program, but it takes time and can disrupt the use of our strategy approach. So we have developed software that you can buy to help you compile and present information. The software will do away with the significant effort that used to be required to 'work the data'.

Apart from this overview and a short conclusion, there are ten chapters in this do-it-yourself guide, each focusing on a particular question or topic. Together, these make up the total picture of a business unit strategy. We have made this text easy to read and a first pass through the text should take you no more than three hours and will leave you with a good general understanding of the business unit strategy process. The software can be bought and downloaded from *www.simplystrategy.com* and it follows the structure of the book. You can perform sample activities before you buy the software, just to check it works as well as we say!

Each section in this book explains the basic idea before providing displays and checklists illustrating the points. Wherever possible you should try to reproduce similar displays for your own business. Do not worry if you feel you don't have the information to sketch out your own display: just take your best guess, and then see what insight would follow if your guess were right.

Later, you may want to go back and collect whatever data are necessary to compile a more correct and complete display. It is very important, however, to get the total picture of business unit strategy by imagining what it could be in all its facets. If you stop every time you don't have the answer to a question you will never complete the exercise and will lose interest. If you carry on and see the power of the total process, you will want to go back and make sure your assumptions were correct. So the rule is: first time round, if you don't know the answer, guess!

To illustrate the voyage of strategy development and discovery we will use two examples.

One is a business in the US, which we shall call the United Tea Company (UTC), and which is part of a food and personal care conglomerate. Richard will show how strategy development changed the views of UTC's top executives and we will see whether its chief executive, Jack Mayhew, manages to hang on to his job.

Our second case is a global business unit called Addit Ltd, a company that manufactures vitamins and other ingredients used in foodstuff. This is a London-based business owned by a US investment firm. Peter will discuss how our approach to strategy helped raise Addit's profits. Addit also developed the ability to improve and increase investment in the growth areas where the firm was already strong.

Both cases are real-life case histories but they are disguised to protect the guilty. The stories also highlight how strategy can be developed either top-down, by the chief executive (as at UTC), or more bottom-up, with extensive involvement of employees, as with Addit.

United Tea Company: Can strategy save Jack?

Jack called me up one warm and sunny November day and asked me to visit UTC's Pasadena head office. UTC is one of America's largest suppliers of branded tea, mainly in tagged bags, and part of a conglomerate in branded goods. When I arrived, Jack, an old friend, came straight to the point. 'I can't figure out what's wrong,' he told me. 'We keep growing our sales but our profits hardly go up at all and our ROI [return on investment] keeps slipping. We've missed our budgets in the last two quarters and if I can't explain to Chicago [the conglomerate's head office] what's wrong and how I'm going to fix it, I'm history.' Jack explained that he was a hands-on manager who'd never had much time for 'all that strategy stuff', but he wanted me to sit down with him over a weekend and work out what was going wrong, and whether it could be fixed. As Jack had done me a favour in the past, I agreed to see if I could help.

Addit: Business strategy from the bottom up

Addit advertises itself as a speciality chemical manufacturing company that produces additives which are widely used in human foods and animal feed. Addit makes these additives – such as vitamins, colourants and anti-oxidants – through its chemical processes, and then sells them to customers such as Procter & Gamble and Unilever (or even UTC!), who work them into products that will eventually end up on supermarket shelves. The company has been especially successful with its line of vitamins. These are used in vitamin-supplement pills and – increasingly – to fortify beverages and foods. Also, they are widely used to improve the growth and health of animals for the bio-industry.

Addit is globally active, but its activities are centred in Europe and North America, and the company has only recently entered the fast-growing Asia Pacific market.

Higher management consists of some twenty managers with varied international backgrounds. Although it has had 'down' years, the company has been generally profitable, showing good growth and cash flow. Return on sales (ROS) and capital employed (ROCE) average 8 per cent and 15 per cent respectively – not stellar, but respectable.

▶

Addit did not, perhaps, look in need of a new strategy and it might have continued to operate without one for ages, but change was in the air. Anyone examining supermarket shelves would have noticed the profusion of products containing additives such as vitamins. While Addit was reaping the fruits of this growth, it was meeting new competition – especially from Far Eastern chemical firms undercutting its prices and squeezing its margins. Some Addit managers were asking whether the firm's much vaunted 'specialities' were perhaps commoditizing. If so, Addit might need a new direction.

At this time Addit gained a new managing director, Susan Jones. Sue was a hands-on leader, naturally inquisitive and passionate to make the best of the business and its people. She demanded that decisions be based on facts. She also asked two questions:

◆ *How strong is each of Addit's business positions?*

◆ *What risks are on the horizon?*

Both were simple questions, but hard to answer. Her probing revealed a disturbing lack of understanding as to where and why Addit had been successful. She also uncovered some more immediate problems, such as Addit's very broad product and customer portfolio, with a multitude of low-volume products and customers. These were not adding a lot of sales, but were time-consuming and expensive to serve, straining Addit's manufacturing and logistics operations.

Sue quickly decided that Addit would benefit from a more rigorous analysis. Since I'd worked with her before in similar situations, she called me. Soon I was flying to London.

We have ten questions to ask both you (as you think about your firm) and the managers of our case-history businesses. The first question looks easier than it is. It is also the beginning of wisdom and the foundation of all later strategy.

2

WHAT BUSINESSES ARE YOU IN?

Within your area, there are almost certainly a lot of different businesses – far more than you realize.

The first step in your strategy process is to define these different BUSINESS SEGMENTS – or segments for short.

Why is this important? One of the most glorious insights about life, the universe and everything, is the 80/20 principle (sometimes called the Pareto principle). This states that 80 per cent of the value of any activity is likely to come from 20 per cent of the inputs. Eighty per cent of the value you generate in your work, or come to that, in your home life, is likely to come from the most useful 20 per cent of your time. Eighty per cent of the profits of a firm are likely to come from 20 per cent of its products. Eighty per cent of the value in a book is likely to come from 20 per cent of its pages (this does not stop publishers churning out long books, because we consumers just won't believe that a short book is worth as much as a longer one!). And so on. Most people could add much more value to the world, and be happier, if they worked out what their most productive 20 per cent of activities were, doubled the amount of time spent on these, and cut out most of the rest.

The 80/20 principle applies to business across different dimensions, most importantly to your business segments, your products, and your customers. But before we can apply the principle, we need to know:

◆ *what business segments you are in (the subject of this section); and*

◆ *the true profitability of your business segments, and preferably also of each of your products and customers. This will be covered by the following section.*

Here we'll define your business segments, in two steps:

1. We'll slice up your business into potential segments on the basis of how you and your customers interact.

2. We'll validate the segments you have defined by looking at the competitive situation in each segment.

IDENTIFYING POTENTIAL BUSINESS SEGMENTS

What is a business segment? Intuitively, this is:

◆ *any significant separate product, service or activity, or*

◆ *any product going to one group of customers as opposed to another, or*

◆ *where the main competitor you face is different, or*

◆ *where the relationship between supplier and customer is different, where there are different buying criteria, or where the cost to serve different customers is different, or*

◆ *where a chunk of business may have higher or lower profitability than apparently 'similar' business.*

This is a lot to think about. Let's take some examples. For a publisher, each book is often a separate segment, since its profitability depends on how many copies it sells, and that is largely independent of how many copies of other books are sold. On the other hand, if books by Dan Brown always sell pretty much the same number, then the segment is 'Dan Brown books' rather than his individual titles. Or if a publisher has a popular series of books on similar subjects and they all have similar profitability, that category becomes the segment.

Or think of any country's postal service. Most postal authorities charge the same for delivering a letter, whether it goes to the next street or hundreds of miles away. But for the US post office, letters delivered in New York City comprise a much more profitable segment than those going to a remote rural community.

Different customers for the same product are often different segments. A bacon supplier will get much less from the largest supermarket chains than from smaller chains or independent grocers. A branded tea supplier such as Twining makes far more profit from Twining brand tea than from tea packed for a supermarket's own brand.

Different end applications can be different segments, especially in technical industries. Selling vitamin C for use in fruit juice might well be different from selling the same vitamin C to add to feeds for cows and pigs.

But caution should be used with this approach because it often hides a more fundamental way of segmenting customers. For example, Dell could segment its sales of computers by large companies (who buy for business use), versus to individuals (for private use). Fair enough, but what is really driving this is a difference in buying criteria and purchasing power. Yet for a supplier to Dell, segmenting by these two end applications 'business' and 'private' would probably be a waste of time. Dell will treat the supplier the same in either case, whether its parts end up in a business or a home computer. It would be better to group all these sales in a segment called 'Dell' or 'large computer manufacturers'.

So what we're really looking for are those customers or groups of customers where your exchange with them is different. Any supplier of services to different customers knows that some of them are no trouble, taking the standard product or service with no arguments about price or what is provided, while others require more service and haggle, quibble and are difficult to extract payment from. These customers – the easy ones and the difficult ones – constitute different segments. They have different buying criteria. Examples here could be large supermarkets versus a speciality deli for foodstuff, or multinational corporations versus family-owned industrial firms.

Another element of your segmentation could be to look at market growth and to treat high- and low-growth areas as different segments. Many high-growth segments are significantly more profitable than their lower-growth counterparts because there is a shortage of qualified supply, allowing suppliers to increase prices. In mature markets there may be oversupply, fierce price competition and low profits or even losses.

Different segments can arise if some customers require a basic product (or COMMODITY) to be adapted to their own requirements (a 'special' product). This could simply be the requirement to deliver a product to the customer's locations, or further stages of working on a product to adapt it to the customer's needs, or just an up-market version of the standard product. A higher price will usually be paid for a special product, but the extra price can be significantly more or significantly less than the extra cost (it is usually less), so the special product can be a different segment, with higher (or, usually, lower) profitability.

Many highly successful company strategies are based on innovative ways of segmenting that satisfy customer requirements better or more economically than competitors. It really pays to take the time with your team to discuss openly how the business could look afresh at its customers and business segments.

Segments, then, may be revealed by any of these:

1. different products or services;

2. different buying criteria of customers receiving the same or similar products;

3. different regions receiving the same product, where the cost to serve the different geographical areas is different. (This is often the case for global companies active in North America, Europe, Japan and Asia);

4. different versions or variants of the same product, distinguished by the degree of value added, quality or personal service involved, or different market growth and profitability.

Although it is important to identify your separate segments, you should not go overboard on this and come up with a long list that is unmanageable. Also, potential separate segments may not be actually separate, if it turns out that their characteristics – especially profitability – are so similar to those of other activities that there is no point in singling them out.

Now's the time to start on your strategy by identifying *your* segments!

EXERCISE 1: IDENTIFY YOUR POTENTIAL BUSINESS SEGMENTS

Exercise 1 is for you to make a list of potential business segments defined by the differences in (1) to (4) above, with the value of sales in each segment next to it – if you don't know the precise sales right now, put an estimate or best guess.

Depending on how big and complex your business is, you should have a list of between ten and fifty potential segments. Make sure no segment is smaller than 1 per cent.

You will probably find yourself defining business segments at different levels of hierarchy. We mean by this, as in the example of Jack below, that you define a general business segment such as 'branded tea' and underneath that group more specific sub-segments such as 'US' and 'Europe'. Alternatively, you could start first defining your general business segments by region 'North America', 'Europe' and 'Asia Pacific', after which you would define the same sub-segments for each region, such as 'mainstream tea' or 'fruit tea', then go to an even deeper level of segmentation, e.g. 'branded' and 'private label'.

(If you use our software, you can define segments at each desired level of hierarchy and the software will assign a four-digit code to each segment. This will make the later manipulation of the data easier.) Illustration 2.1 shows an example of business segments at different levels, with their codes.

EXERCISE 2: ARE THE SEGMENTS REALLY SEPARATE?

Exercise 2 turns this guesswork into a more objective definition of business segments.

We have compiled two tests that can be used for this validation. Begin by taking two possible segments, that could be separate segments, or that could just be one bigger segment. Imagine you're a butcher owning two shops, one in Madrid and the other in Barcelona. You want to know whether you should think of them as separate business segments.

The two tests are alternatives: Test A is a short, quick-and-dirty test that will probably give you the right answer. Test B is longer and more certain to be

ILLUSTRATION 2.1

Example of a hierarchy of coded business segments

No.	Code	Segment
	2000	Human nutrition
	2100	Vitamins
	2110	*Food & beverages*
1	2111	Americas
2	2112	Europe
3	2113	Asia-Pacific
4	2120	*Supplements*
	2200	Colors
5	2210	*Food*
6	2220	*Beverages*
7	2230	*Pharmaceuticals*

correct. (You can do both tests by hand, but if you have defined your segments using our software, the program will define a table that will allow you to carry out either Test A, or B, or both for all the relevant segments you have defined.)

TEST A: QUICK-AND-DIRTY

Test A asks two simple questions:

1. Are your competitors in the two potential business segments different or the same? If the answer to this question is 'different', then they are probably separate segments, and you do not need to answer question 2.

2. If the answer to question 1 is 'the same', do the competitors (including your firm) have roughly similar market share positions in the two potential business segments? In other words, if Competitor A is the leader in one potential segment, followed by B, followed by C, is this the same ranking in the other potential segment? *If so, the two areas are probably one single segment; if not, they are probably separate segments.*

To go back to the Spanish butcher, if his rivals in Madrid are different from those in Barcelona, he should think of the two shops as different segments. If both shops were next door to the same supermarket chain and the butcher reckoned that the supermarket was his most important competitor, his two shops would be one segment.

Take another example: a furniture manufacturer in Transylvania has two main product lines: sofas and sofa-beds. His main competitor is Dracula Sofas, which also makes sofa-beds. Question 1 produces the answer 'the same', since both firms make sofas and sofa-beds. But in the answer to question 2, we discover the market shares shown in Illustration 2.2.

Our firm has only half the market share and sales in sofas that Dracula Sofas has, but has five times the market share of Dracula in sofa-beds, which is clearly our firm's speciality and not Dracula's.

We need to introduce a piece of jargon here, which is the RELATIVE MARKET SHARE (RMS). The relative market share is simply your firm's market share divided by the market share of your largest competitor. If you are larger than anyone else in a product, your RMS will be more than 1.0 (written as 1.0x or 1x); if you are smaller it will be less than 1, as in the example above in sofas where our firm is half the size of Dracula; this is written as 0.5x.

We conclude, that the relative market share positions in sofas are different from those in sofa-beds, so we should therefore treat them as separate segments. Our firm specializes in sofa-beds and Dracula specializes in sofas. There must be good reasons for this difference, which are likely to result in different profitability. The chances are that our firm will be much more profitable in sofa-beds than in sofas, and more profitable than Dracula in sofa-beds. Conversely, Dracula is likely to make more money out of sofas than sofa-beds, and to have a higher return on sales in sofas but a lower return on sales in sofa-beds than we do.

Why should it matter whether the competitive positions are the same? The reason is that if they are the same, it says that the way customers vote, and the ability of the two competitors to produce one product rather than another, is not much different in the two areas. The chances are, therefore, that Competitor A will have similar levels of profitability in each area, and that the same will be true for Competitor B (Competitor A is likely to be either more profitable, or less profitable, than Competitor B in both areas). But if one competitor is a

ILLUSTRATION 2.2

Transylvanian sofa and sofa-bed market shares

	Sofas	Sofa-beds
Our firm's market share	30%	50%
Dracula Sofas' market share	60%	10%
Our firm's relative market share	0.5x	5x

specialist in one area, and has a higher market share in that area, there is likely to be something in consumers' preferences, or the firm's own ability to produce efficiently in one area, that means one segment is likely to be more profitable than the other.

Even if the profitability of two segments is not different, the fact that a firm is relatively stronger in market share terms in one area than another indicates that this could be the basis of profitable specialization.

Relative market share is extremely useful in business unit strategy. For one thing, it greatly reduces the data collection and effort necessary. Many companies do too much analysis. They define the market share not only of themselves and the largest competitor but also of the other important players. Yet defining the market share of these additional players requires a lot of extra work and is usually not terribly useful. Imagine you are a small, 5 per cent player among six others in an industry, and the market leader commands 45 per cent of share. The dynamics of the market follow what the market leader does. The market shares of the other competitors are largely irrelevant. Alternatively, if you are the market leader with 15 per cent share, and your only large rival has 14 per cent, then your roughly 1x RMS tells all about the dynamics in the industry and how the customer votes. Essentially there are two equally preferred suppliers and your leeway for improving your position depends not only on what you do but also on the actions of this competitor. RMS does away with a lot of effort establishing the market shares of players that really don't really matter.

TEST B: SEGMENTATION MINCER

Test B, to see whether segments are separate, takes longer than Test A but is even more reliable – though it usually comes up with the same result. We recommend you use this test in two cases: (1) when you are not too certain about your RMS in the segments, or (2) when the outcome of Test A results remains in doubt or there are different opinions among your team members.

We start with the same question – we have two product lines or potential segments, and we want to know whether they are part of the same segment, or comprise two different segments. Illustration 2.3 gives the tests for what some irreverent junior consultants once called the 'segmentation mincer'. (You can fill out this very same checklist for each two segments using our software.)

Let us take the segmentation mincer and apply it to our friend, the Spanish butcher. Remember that he has two shops, one in Madrid and one in Barcelona, and he is trying to find out whether he is in two businesses, two competitive systems if you like, or just one.

ILLUSTRATION 2.3

The segmentation mincer

	Column A score	Column B score
1. Are the competitors in the two products or areas the same? Yes: Column A No: Column B	–30	+30
2. Are the relative market shares (RMS) of our firm and the leading competitors roughly the same in the two products or areas? RMS similar: Column A RMS different Column B	–50	+50
3. Are the customers the same in the two products or areas? Yes: Column A No: Column B	–20	+20
4. Are the customers' main purchase criteria and their order of importance roughly the same in the two products or areas? Yes: Column A No: Column B	–30	+30
5. Are the two products substitutes for each other? Yes: Column A No: Column B	–10	+10
6. Are the prices of the two products (for equivalent quality) or in the two areas roughly the same? Yes: Column A No: Column B	–20	+20
7. Is our firm's profitability roughly the same in the two products or areas? Yes: Column A No: Column B	–40	+40
8. Do the two products or areas have approximately the same need for capital per unit values of sales, i.e. similar capital intensity? Yes: Column A No: Column B	–10	+10
9. Are the cost structures in the two products or areas similar (that is, roughly the same proportion of cost in raw materials, in manufacturing, in marketing and selling, and so on)? Yes: Column A No: Column B	–10	+10
10. Do the products or areas share at least half of their costs, that is, the use of common labor, machines, premises and management resources for at least half of their total costs? Yes: Column A No: Column B	–30	+30
11. Are there logistical, practical or technological barriers between the two products or areas that only some competitors can surmount? No: Column A Yes: Column B	+20	–20
12. Is it possible to gain an economical advantage by specializing in one of the products/areas by gaining lower costs or higher prices in that product/area as a result of focusing on it? No: Column A Yes: Column B	+30	–30

You now add the scores together to produce the result. If the result is a positive number, you should treat the two products or areas as separate business segments, and devise a strategy for each of them separately. If the result is negative, they are currently the same business segment and should be lumped together, at least initially, in developing their strategy. The further away from zero the answer is, whether positive or negative, the more certain the result.

ILLUSTRATION 2.4

The Spanish butcher uses the mincer

		Answer	Score
1.	Are the competitors in Madrid and Barcelona the same?	No	+30
2.	Are the Relative Market Shares of the competitors the same in Madrid and Barcelona?	No	+50
3.	Are the customers the same?	No	+20
4.	Are the customers' purchase criteria roughly the same?	Yes	−30
5.	Are the two shops substitutes for each other (i.e. would a customer sometimes shop in Barcelona and sometimes in Madrid)?	No	+10
6.	Are the prices for the same products roughly the same?	Yes	−20
7.	Is the butcher's profitability in the two locations similar?	Yes	−40
8.	Do the two shops have the same capital intensity (need for capital per euro of sales)?	Yes	−10
9.	Are the cost structures similar?	Yes	−10
10.	Do the two locations share at least half their costs?	No	+30
11.	Are there barriers between competitors participating in both areas?	Yes	+20
12.	Can you gain an economic advantage by just competing in one area	Yes	+30
Total score			**+80**

The result is +80, indicating that the two shops are different business segments and that the butcher should therefore develop a strategy for each shop, as well as a strategy for the business overall.

Using the software, both Test A and the segmentation mincer can be easily done for each business segment combination. If you find that two segments are the same, you can combine them in your list of segments, and a new table will be generated by the program, with one fewer segment. You can continue this iterative process for each segment combination until it has been established that each segment is separate from each other, and you are satisfied with the final picture.

Now let's return to UTC in Pasadena and to Addit in London to see how Jack Mayhew and Sue Jones are defining their business segments.

Jack defines UTC's business segments

As you've probably gathered, Jack is a busy, no-nonsense guy. When I told him we were going to define his business segments, he sighed, but reluctantly switched his cell phone off. 'I don't think we need too long,' he said. 'We have three businesses, or maybe four. Our biggest business by far, with over $700m of sales, is the Mainstream Tea business under the 5 Unicorns brand. Simply put, we buy tea from plantations around the world, we put it into tea-bags, we put tags on the ends of the bags, we box them up with pretty packaging and we sell them to the grocery trade, especially to the big supermarkets.'

'You can split this business into two if you want. The US business is tough. We have nearly $600m of sales revenue, but we make almost nothing out of it. We used to make a fair return, nothing great, but now the supermarket chains have tightened up on us and are squeezing our margins. Fortunately, the export business keeps us alive: we make $8.5m pre-tax out of revenues of between just $115m and $120m, something like that.'

'Then we have two smaller businesses, but growing fast. One is Herb Tea. That's just $65m in revenues, but we make even more at the bottom line out of that than the Mainstream Tea exports. Finally there's the latest craze, Fruit Tea, and we make $3m profit out of just under $30m revenue. We bought these two businesses a couple of years ago and they're still separate. If I hadn't done those two deals, I'd be on welfare by now.'

Knowing that businessmen often misquote numbers, I asked to see last year's management accounts. But in this case, they proved that Jack was right (see Illustration 2.5).

'It's difficult to make money out of tea in the US. We've put all our development effort into increasing our export sales and profits. The exports deliver, but our advances here are overturned by the slide in domestic margins. Herb and fruit teas are very profitable and growing, and we have been successful in exports, which must also be the most profitable bit of the business.'

Jack was convinced that he had just four business segments, as in the accounts below. But I was not sure.

'Let's start with the Mainstream Tea domestic business,' I probed. 'Are there any chunks of the business where you face different competition, or have higher or lower margins, than the rest?'

'No, not really. Not unless you count the private label stuff we do for two of the supermarkets. It's true we're up against specialist players there, you know,

ILLUSTRATION 2.5
UTC's previous report

Organizational unit	Sales $m	Profit ($000)	ROS% (return on sales)
Mainstream Tea US	589.6	233	0.0
Mainstream Tea Exports	117.2	8,510	7.3
Herb Tea Corporation	66.5	8,870	13.3
Fruit Tea Corporation	27.9	3,249	11.6
Total	801.2	20,862	2.6

commodity firms with no brands and no marketing overheads. Our biggest headache there is a guy we call Cheapco, because he always undercuts us for the Big Boy Supermarkets contract, or so Big Boy tells us.'

'Doesn't that make the private label business less profitable than the branded business?' Jack had to pause before answering, a rare event. 'Well, maybe. But the branded business is no great shakes anyway. We're dealing with the supermarkets in both cases, and they're real SOBS.'

Despite Jack's reservations, I was convinced that private label business was a separate segment, because the main competitor was different. To cut a long story short, I pressed my advantage and discovered that there was another private label contract, for Small Fry Retailers, a contract that Cheapco did not try to win, because it was too small. The main competitor here was another commodity player, and I marked the Small Fry business down as another potential segment.

I was also unhappy at the way Jack lumped all the exports for the main-stream tea business together. Didn't he face different competitors in Canada, in Europe and in the rest of the world (ROW)? 'Half right,' he conceded. 'In Europe and ROW the main competitor is the same as here, United Foods, but in Canada it's a local outfit, Canadian Tea'. I wrote down 'Canada' as a separate segment, but was not yet willing to give up on having Europe and the rest of the world as separate too. 'How big are you relative to United Foods,' I asked, 'here, in Europe and in the rest of the world?' 'Well, we're the biggest at home, but much smaller than they are in Europe. Heck, United Foods is based in Switzerland. In ROW, though, we're several times their size, which is stronger even than in the US; they're probably about three quarters our size here in branded tea, though they don't do private label.'

This confirmed my suspicion: with United Foods and UTC taking different positions, ROW and Europe must be different segments. I then asked similar questions about competitors in herb tea and fruit tea. It emerged that in both markets there were different foreign competitors, though one firm (Auntie Dot's) was the main competitor in the export markets for both herb and fruit teas.

I could see that Jack was getting itchy and sure enough, he suggested we take a break. While he made a few phone calls I wrote down my idea of UTC's segments. Instead of his three or four segments, I thought there were at least ten:

1. Branded (5 Unicorns) Tea: US
2. Branded (5 Unicorns) Tea: Canada
3. Branded (5 Unicorns) Tea: Europe
4. Branded (5 Unicorns) Tea: ROW
5. Big Boy Supermarkets private label
6. Small Fry Retailers private label
7. Herb Tea: US
8. Herb Tea: Exports
9. Fruit Tea: US
10. Fruit Tea: Exports

After his calls, Jack agreed that we could use these ten segments and he left to visit a customer.

Addit and its segments

Like so many companies, Addit's managers had a good intuitive sense of the main segments they were active in, but had never carefully defined them. When I asked Sue and her team, they quickly came up with ten main business segments for total sales of some £280 million. However, they didn't track their sales according to these segments, nor could they split their £21.4 million profit between them.

Addit was used to working as three rather separate, regional organizations: Americas, Europe and Asia Pacific. Each used a different terminology for markets and types of customers. This had worked OK in the past, but Sue noted that Addit's business was becoming more global, with important customers setting up shop in two or more regions. She wanted Addit to adopt a global approach with standardized segment definitions everywhere.

I started the segmentation process at a meeting with Paul, the European marketing manager, and his sales executives. Paul and his colleagues tended to define segments in terms of products and their final uses. Technical companies such as

Addit like to do this – after all this is their world, providing technical solutions by selling a product for a specific use. For example, Addit makes anti-oxidants, a common additive in food and beverages to keep food fresh. So we grouped all Addit's anti-oxidant sales into one segment, which with stunning originality we called 'Anti-oxidants'. These are commodities – everybody gets the same price and very little technical support is necessary. So this made good sense to me.

But sometimes just looking at your products doesn't tell you the whole story, and in the case of vitamins, we had to go a little further. Vitamins are used in food, drinks, vitamin supplements, cosmetics and animal feeds. In foodstuffs, we realized that there was a difference between food and beverages, on the one hand, versus supplements, on the other hand. In food and beverage, Addit's customers were consumer goods companies, but in supplements the customers were pharmaceutical firms. So these had to be different segments.

And some of the vitamins sales end up in personal care products, together with other compounds. Here we found that what really mattered was not which product Addit sold (a vitamin, a colouring), or its final use (foodstuffs, supplements) but rather to whom – the cosmetics industry.

What about the vitamins that Addit uses in animal feed? In addition to vitamins, Addit sells two other products: stabilizers and amino acids. Initially we took these as our segments. But while talking about this, we realized that for each of these products Addit is dealing with three types of customers: large multinational feed manufacturers; smaller 'pre-mixers'; and consumer-type companies making pet-food. Each of these customers buys vitamins, stabilizers and amino acids (a 'package sell') but each has unique requirements. The large feed manufacturers buy and sell product in bulk and are tough on price. The smaller 'pre-mixers' buy smaller volumes, and because they have less clout and need more technical support they pay more. And the pet food companies' product usually ends up on supermarket shelves, making the pet food customers similar to the food multinationals. Much better then to segment the animal feed area by customer type than by product.

So over the course of half a day we came up with about thirty segments. We did not stick to one way of segmenting. We tried to find out with each other what aspects about Addit's customers were most important, what defined its market. Sometimes the product view mattered most (a sweetener, an anti-oxidant), but at other times we found the buyer was more important (the pet food industry). In yet other instances we used a mix of the two (vitamins, to the food and beverages customers).

We sent our list to Paul's US counterpart, Hank. Hank was an industry veteran and he suggested some changes appropriate for his market. He also combined some of the smaller segments on the basis of the competitive situation in the US using Tests A and B. This resulted in a list of twenty-two segments, which Addit's global business team approved without changes. Illustration 2.6 shows the final result.

ILLUSTRATION 2.6

Business segmentation for Addit

Nr.	Code	Segment
	1000	**Animal Nutrition**
1	1100	Pet foods
2	1200	Pre-mixers
3	1300	Integrated manufacturers
	2000	**Human Nutrition**
	2100	Vitamins
4	*2110*	*Food & Beverages*
5	*2120*	*Supplements*
	2200	Colors
6	*2210*	*Food*
7	*2220*	*Beverages*
8	*2230*	*Pharmaceuticals*
9	2300	Anti-oxidants
10	2400	Sweeteners
11	2500	New extracts
12	2600	Other human nutrition
13	**3000**	**Personal Care**
	4000	**Nutritional Blends**
14	4100	Proprietary blends
15	4200	Custom blends
16	4300	Standard blends
	5000	**Other**
17	5100	Intermediates
18	5200	Plastic additives
19	5300	Non-food citric acid
20	5400	Paint additives
21	5500	Specialities
22	5600	Distributors

So in a matter of weeks and a few meetings, Sue and her team had successfully completed the first step of developing their business strategy: a new, improved segmentation of Addit's regional markets, using global names and definitions. Note that each of Addit's regions will serve all twenty-two segments, which means that Addit, on a global basis, has three × twenty-two or sixty-six actual business segments. Here, for ease of reading, we show only a globally consolidated list, but bear in mind that Addit's managers look at these twenty-two segments regionally to develop their strategy.

There are three points that come out of Illustration 2.6. First, note that Addit has defined four segments categories, what they call 'macro segments': animal nutrition, human nutrition, personal care, and nutritional blends. Then it combines a lot of smaller products and activities in a macro segment called other. This is a common pattern. A business has several main business lines and then a couple of 'cats and dogs' outside of those main lines, which are grouped together in a basket with a non-specific label such as 'other' or, more flattering but not much more informative, 'specialities'. Often, the existence of such an area is a clue for possible poor profitability.

Second, note that under other, Addit defines a segment called distributors. These are firms that sell Addit's products to small customers or in countries where Addit has no sales representatives. True, these sales ultimately end up in areas such as human nutrition and animal nutrition, and you might think therefore that they should be made part of those areas. But Addit is correct in singling distributors out. Distributors form a distinct group of customers, with different buying behaviour and different costs in serving them. Probably, they are significantly more or less profitable than other sales for nutritional end uses.

Third, Addit isolates a fast-growth segment called new extracts (which has great potential but is not yet profitable).

We agreed that Addit's sales executives would assign each of their sales to one of the twenty-two business segments, and assess each segment's profitability. We'll see the results in the next chapter.

You probably already have the idea by now, but in case you are in any doubt let's give one more example (skip this if you are confident you know how to 'mince'). Two firms, which we shall call Heinz and Imperial Foods, are manufacturers of sauces. They both make tomato ketchup and thick brown sauce. One of the firms wishes to know whether they are separate business segments for strategy purposes. At first sight it appears obvious that they are the same segment, because the main competitors are the same and because there is very high cost-sharing between the two types of sauce: they are made in the same factories, using the same machines, by the same workforce; they are marketed to the same consumers and sold to the same customers (the supermarkets and other grocers) by the same sales force. Nevertheless, it is useful to put these two potential segments through the mincer (Illustration 2.7).

ILLUSTRATION 2.7

Is tomato ketchup the same segment as thick brown sauce?

Test		Answer	Score
1.	Are the competitors the same in the two sauces?	Yes	–30
2.	Are the relative market shares of the competitors roughly the same in the two sauces?	No	+50
3.	Are the customers the same?	Yes	–20
4.	Are the customers' purchasing criteria roughly the same?	Yes	–30
5.	Are the two sauces substitutes for each other?	No	+10
6.	Are the prices for the two products roughly the same between the two competitors, with no brand premium?	No	+20
7.	Is Imperial Foods' (or Heinz's) profitability in the two sauces similar?	No	+40
8.	Do the two products have similar capital intensity?	Yes	–10
9.	Are the cost structures similar?	Yes	–10
10.	Do the two sauces share at least half their costs?	Yes	–30
11.	Are there barriers stopping one firm or the other from competing as effectively in one sauces as in the other?	Yes	+20
12.	Can you gain an economic advantage by competing in just one sauce?	Yes	+30
Total score			**+40**

The results is +40, indicating that, contrary to first impressions, the two sauces are separate business segments.

We need to explain why the questions were answered as they were. Heinz is the market leader in tomato ketchup, several times larger than the nearest competitor. But in thick brown sauces (under several brands, including Daddies), Imperial Foods is the market leader, where it is several times larger than anyone else. There is no particularly good reason for this difference, except (and it is a big 'except') that consumers are attached to the brands, Heinz in tomato ketchup and Daddies in brown sauce. The consumers obstinately and persistently vote massive majorities for the two brands in each of their areas. This has the result that Heinz commands a high brand price premium in tomato ketchup, and Daddies enjoys the same higher price in brown sauce because of the strength of the brand. Consequently, Heinz is very profitable in ketchup (but not in brown sauce), whereas Imperial Foods is very profitable in brown sauce and not in ketchup. Each area therefore deserves a separate strategy, with separate pricing and differential degrees of brand support. It would be wrong for either firm to treat both products as part of one sauce business and have the same strategy in each area.

The segmentation mincer does not always say businesses are separate segments! If red sauce is a separate segment, what about red cars? Clearly no-one can command a price premium or have lower costs by specializing in producing red cars today, so the mincer would produce a high negative score (actually the maximum possible negative score, -290).

SUMMARY

So, to come back to your business, the first step towards a strategy is to define your business segments. Take some time out to look again at your market and make a list of potential business segments. Next, apply Test A or the mincer to your list to arrive at a list of 'real' business segments. If you can, add their sales revenues.

Try to answer the questions posed by each of the following chapters for each segment, either doing it one segment at a time (starting with the most important segments) or doing all segments at once.

3

WHERE DO YOU MAKE THE MONEY?

Now that you've defined your business in a new way, by its real business segments, the most important thing to know is which of these segments generates most of your profits, both in terms of absolute amounts of money and in terms of profitability (measured by return on sales (ROS), or, preferably, return on capital employed (ROCE), sometimes also called return on investment, or ROI).

It may be that your accounting system already provides this information, or can be easily tweaked to do so. If so, great. It's more likely, however, that the profits for the segments you have just defined are not readily available. One reason could be that you've not been tracking your performance according to this new definition. It could also be that you simply don't track your performance at such a detailed level. But such tracking is essential if you want to develop a sound strategy.

At this point you can choose between two pathways.

Path A is to *estimate* your segment profitability as best as you can, using a top-down approach. This path is fast and quite revealing. Its downsides are that it does not challenge any conventional wisdom or prejudice that may exist in your business and it does not provide information beyond business segments.

Path B involves a much more rigorous *bottom-up* approach that will identify the profitability of your individual sales, then aggregate them into their appropriate business segments. This approach requires some effort, but will result in a very powerful 'fingerprint' of your business – showing profitability not just by business segment, but also by individual product and customer.

PATH A: TOP-DOWN ESTIMATE

Start by identifying all the available accounting information. You will certainly be able to discover your sales per segment. Probably, you will know the procurement or raw material costs for each of the products that you make. This gives the contribution margin (sales less cost of goods).

You will also know your total costs for all the segments, including your manufacturing costs (or costs of production, bringing you the gross margin), and your costs for sales and distribution, general and administrative and research and development, together called SG&A or SAR costs. You may also know the profitability of certain segments on an aggregated basis – all of UTC's Unicorn brand teas, for example, even if you can't yet split the US costs from Canada's costs. Now all you need to do, to arrive at the return on sales for each segment, is to allocate the costs to each segment in a reasonable way.

Illustration 2.8 gives the steps by which profit (or operating income) is derived from net sales. This is also known as the P&L (profit and loss) line.

The crudest way of allocating costs is by percentage of turnover (or total sales), and you could start by just doing this. A moment's reflection, however, will convince you that this is not terribly accurate. Some products take a lot more of particular costs than others – more advertising, for example, or more time selling, or more cost in the factory because the production runs are shorter.

ILLUSTRATION 2.8

Arriving at profit and loss for a business

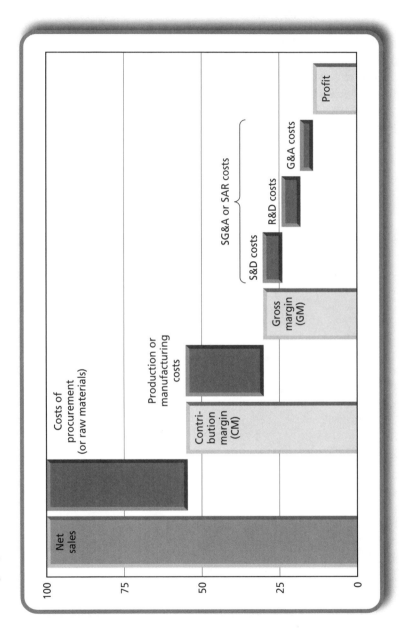

Take each major category of cost, however arranged in your accounting system, and make a rough allocation of costs to each segment. Start with the simplest product, the one easiest to make and sell, and give it a cost of y per unit of product in the particular department you are looking at – making it your reference product. Then ask how much more difficult it is to make the next product – $1.5y$ for example, or $2y$, or $10y$. Do the same for each other product, then multiply the factor ($1.5y$ or whatever) by the volume of that product. Go through the same procedure for all other products, add up the total number of ys, and then allocate the departmental cost based on each product's ys divided into the total number of ys.

Analyzing UTC's profits

Back in Pasadena, Jack's accountant and I spent Saturday afternoon beavering away to turn UTC's previous profit numbers for four businesses (see page 25) into profits split by the ten new segments, while Jack went off on a long-standing golfing obligation. Shortly after ten at night, we were satisfied that we had it about right (see Illustrations 2.9 and 2.10).

ILLUSTRATION 2.9
UTC's profit numbers after proper segmentation

UTC segment profitability

Segment	Sales ($m)	Profit ($000)	ROS%
5 Unicorns brand: US	200.1	17,800	8.9
5 Unicorns brand: Canada	23.7	1,232	5.2
5 Unicorns brand: Europe	45.0	1,215	2.7
5 Unicorns brand: ROW	48.5	6,063	12.5
Private label for Big Boy Supermarkets	353.6	(18,034)	(5.1)
Private label for Small Fry Retailers	35.9	467	1.3
Herb Tea US	55.5	7,715	13.9
Herb Tea Exports	11.0	1,155	10.5
Fruit Tea US	23.2	2,784	12.0
Fruit Tea Exports	4.7	465	9.9
Total	**801.2**	**20,862**	**2.6**

The following morning, I went through the numbers with Jack. He was stunned. 'You mean to say that we really do make good money out of the domestic branded business, but lose it all on the private label contracts? And that the US brand is more profitable than Canada or Europe? That's amazing! Perhaps we can do things to get even more branded sales here. But I don't know what to do about the private label contracts. You may tell me to cut them out, but they're too big a part of our business and they still make a contribution to my overheads.'

We agreed not to jump to conclusions until we had gone through my other questions.

ILLUSTRATION 2.10
UTC's sales breakdown

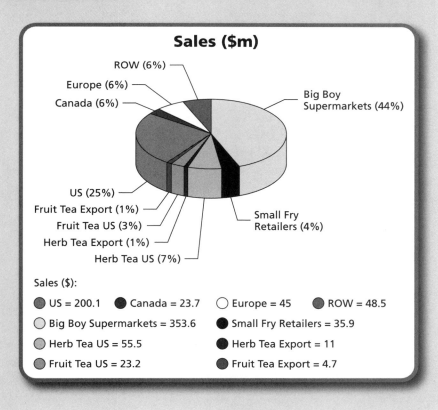

Sales ($m)

ROW (6%)
Europe (6%)
Canada (6%)
Big Boy Supermarkets (44%)
US (25%)
Fruit Tea Export (1%)
Fruit Tea US (3%)
Herb Tea Export (1%)
Herb Tea US (7%)
Small Fry Retailers (4%)

Sales ($):
- US = 200.1
- Canada = 23.7
- Europe = 45
- ROW = 48.5
- Big Boy Supermarkets = 353.6
- Small Fry Retailers = 35.9
- Herb Tea US = 55.5
- Herb Tea Export = 11
- Fruit Tea US = 23.2
- Fruit Tea Export = 4.7

Before long we'll have a rough-and-ready estimate of the product's return on sales. (You can use the software to organize the information and generate some useful graphs.) If you want to take this to the stage of return on capital – which is nearly always very useful – follow a similar procedure to allocate the capital used by each product or segment.

(If you are using the software, enter your profit information in the appropriate table to output analysis and graphs later on.)

PATH B: BOTTOM-UP OR PROFITABILITY FINGERPRINTING

The concept behind profitability fingerprinting is easy enough. Take all of your sales to all customers and allocate all of your costs across those sales. Doing this will give you detailed profitability information in every conceivable way: by product, by customer, by business segment, by geography, etc. Moreover, because you'll need to involve many of your people in the process, the whole company will be much more aware of the effect of everyone's activities.

Start by compiling a list of each of last-year's *product-customer combinations*. A product-customer combination is the sale of one particular product to one particular customer. Selling another product to the same customer would be a different product-customer combination. (If you sell services rather than tangible products, read 'service' whenever we refer to products.)

You might wonder why we don't simply segment at the global level of 'product' or 'customer'. The trouble is that this wouldn't be very accurate. Addit, for example, sells identical vitamins to pharmaceutical customers as to the food and drink industry. We've already established that these are different segments. Similarly, the same customer can be active in different segments, for example in both human food and beverage and pet food. Clearly it is the *combination* of product and customer that matters.

A list of all of last year's product-customer combinations is likely to be available from your company's sales records. Most likely, too, for each of these customer-product combinations you will have the cost of goods required to make your finished product. From here you can derive contribution margin (CM). Since it is so easy to come by, CM is used a lot to guide business decisions. But as we shall see for Addit, it is a bad measure for true profit, sending many companies astray.

It's a good idea now to involve more of your colleagues, starting with the sales executives. Send them a list of the product-customer combinations they are responsible for, and ask them to segment each of these using the new business segmentation. This process is shown in Illustration 2.11, where all your customer-product combinations (and later, the costs associated with them) are assigned to their specific segment. You'll then be able to aggregate the net sales and CM of all product-customer combinations into their overall categories. Stand by for a surprise or two!

ILLUSTRATION 2.11

Segmenting individual sales and their associated raw material costs

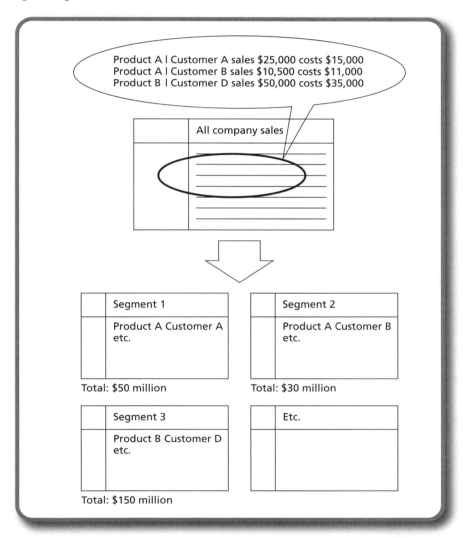

Addit gets a first impression

Addit's sales managers received a list with their customer-product combinations drawn directly from Addit's sales records. We also provided them with the new business segments and asked them to assign each customer-product combination to a segment. Two weeks later the results were back, and were aggregated to show sales and contribution margin, by business segment (Illustration 2.12). We drew two pie charts – Illustrations 2.13 and 2.14.

ILLUSTRATION 2.12

Addit net sales and contribution margin by segment

Code	Segment	Net sales (£m)	Contribution margin (£m)	CM%	% of total NS	% of total CM
1000	**Animal nutrition**	**48,296**	**18,497**	**38%**	**17%**	**16%**
1100	Pet food	13,717	4,895	36%		
1200	Pre-mixers	21,262	8,730	41%		
1300	Integrated manufacturers	13,318	4,871	37%		
2000	**Human nutrition**	**107,137**	**47,986**	**45%**	**39%**	**42%**
2100	Vitamins	42,615	19,431	46%		
2110	*Food & beverages*	*16,127*	*7,604*	*47%*		
2120	*Supplements*	*26,488*	*11,826*	*45%*		
2200	Colors	30,362	12,765	42%		
2210	*Food*	*14,132*	*5,998*	*42%*		
2220	*Beverages*	*10,965*	*4,536*	*41%*		
2230	*Pharmaceuticals*	*5,266*	*2,232*	*42%*		
2300	Anti-oxidants	3,991	1,400	35%		
2400	Sweeteners	18,811	9,614	51%		
2500	New extracts	5,186	1,991	38%		
2600	Other human nutrition	6,172	2,785	45%		
3000	**Personal care**	**25,588**	**6,622**	**26%**	**9%**	**6%**
4000	**Nutritional blends**	**20,778**	**13,295**	**64%**	**8%**	**12%**
4100	Proprietary blends	8,831	6,658	75%		
4200	Custom blends	5,076	3,259	64%		
4300	Standard blends	6,871	3,379	49%		
5000	**Other**	**75,062**	**27,508**	**37%**	**27%**	**24%**
5100	Intermediates	22,144	10,590	48%		
5200	Plastic additives	11,713	2,917	25%		
5300	Non-food citric acid	14,567	5,451	37%		
5400	Paint additives	5,992	910	15%		
5500	Specialities	4,263	1,916	45%		
5600	Distributors	16,383	5,724	35%		
Total		**276,861**	**113,909**	**41%**		

ILLUSTRATION 2.13

Addit's sales by revenue (£m) and percentage for the main segments

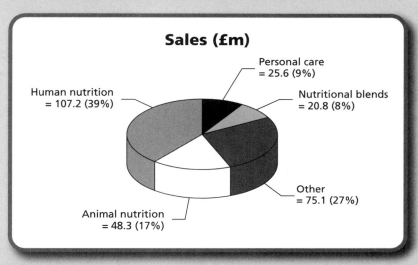

Sales (£m)

Personal care = 25.6 (9%)

Human nutrition = 107.2 (39%)

Nutritional blends = 20.8 (8%)

Other = 75.1 (27%)

Animal nutrition = 48.3 (17%)

ILLUSTRATION 2.14

Addit's contribution margin (£m) by main segment

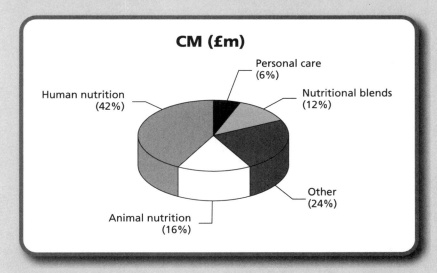

CM (£m)

Personal care (6%)

Human nutrition (42%)

Nutritional blends (12%)

Other (24%)

Animal nutrition (16%)

The new segmentation showed that almost 39 per cent of sales were generated by the human nutrition business. Since sales were previously tracked by product rather than segment, Addit management had not realized how reliant it was on this business segment. Executives were also surprised by the rather large chunk of 'Other' business – more than a quarter of the total being outside Addit's core activities, with low contribution margin.

Measured by contribution margin, human nutrition was even more important. The low margin in personal care was less surprising. With less regulation, ingredients in this area do not need to be as pure as the ingredients for foods and feeds. Addit faced a lot more low-end competition in this segment. Nor was the higher contribution from blends a surprise, given the higher prices Addit was able to charge.

The big question now was how these findings would change after analysis to determine profit.

The next step is to subtract costs of manufacturing (production costs) from the contribution margin to derive your gross margin (GM). The GM is the money you make on a product once it leaves your factory or service department, but before the costs for selling, developing new products, and management overheads are subtracted. The idea is to find out what it costs to produce each of your products or services and then allocate those costs to each product-customer combination. Your colleagues and employees in manufacturing and/or in customer service will probably know what these costs are for the different products and services, and may well already have a system to track and allocate costs.

But even if they do, make sure that everyone agrees on a sensible way to allocate these costs. This is especially the case in manufacturing industries where plants are large cost centres and production lines are shared between different products. You can do this simply by asking your manufacturing colleagues to explain to your team their rationale and system for allocation. While this is not a trival exercise, you can be sure it will teach you a lot about your business. Plus, you may well decide on some meaningful improvements.

After allocating manufacturing costs, move on to allocate the SG&A or SAR costs. These costs must be allocated to each product/service combination.

How is this to be done? Well, each sales manager should be able to allocate his own costs (salary and overheads) based on the basis of the time spent on each customer-product combination. The manager of the order department responsible for shipping material from your company to customers can split out the department's costs by the number of orders (maybe taking into account the relative complexity of difficult export against easier local orders). Advertising campaigns can probably be specifically allocated to the product advertised. The R&D manager can allocate costs to the product or customer group they support. Technical service can probably be allocated to the specific customers or product it was related to. Finally, tackle overhead costs such as senior management salaries and the costs of the controlling department. These are not easily allocated to specific customers or products on an activity basis. You could do this simply by turnover or CM.

You will find there is no shortage of ways to allocate costs and every type of cost will probably warrant its own specific way. Sometimes, company guidelines may provide useful input. Whatever you decide, take time with your people to go through these principles and achieve agreement. But don't go overboard. Focus on the main cost 'buckets' and encourage your people to focus on the main cost 'drivers' when allocating costs to those buckets.

The last step is to determine the capital employed to supply your products or services. This has two components:

◆ *capital invested in physical assets, such as factories and manufacturing equipment; and*

◆ *working capital – the sum of inventory and accounts payable, less accounts receivable.*

Capital invested in equipment and plants may usually be best allocated in a similar way to manufacturing costs, taking into account the products it is employed for. Accounts payable and receivable may be allocated to customers or to products depending on what really drives these costs in your business.

Illustration 2.15 depicts the process, showing several customer-product combinations, and where their associated costs come from. The figure doesn't show the full details. For example, the SAR costs you see are an aggregation of more detailed allocations. But you'll get the general idea, and see that contribution margin, as straightforward to get and easy to use as it is, can be highly deceptive.

ILLUSTRATION 2.15

Results of cost allocation for each product-customer combination

Country	Account manager	Customer	Product	Segment	Sales (tonnes)	Sales (£)	CM (£)	CM%	FMC (£)	GM (£)	Total S&D	Total R&D	Total G&A	Total SAR	Profit	ROS	Capital Invested	ROI
USA	Kathy D	Lieberman Inc.	Vitamin B	2110	38.0	85,378	49,197	58%	12,360	36,837	6,460	1,708	2,323	10,491	26,346	31%	20,775	127%
USA	Kathy D	FFC Inc.	Vitamin A	2110	12.8	40,934	17,852	44%	2,415	15,438	8,212	1,999	1,114	11,325	4,112	10%	6,998	50%
China	UPU	Zhongdu Company	Vitamin C	2110	210.0	533,819	252,065	47%	30,428	221,638	33,897	14,082	14,526	62,506	159,132	30%	114,809	139%
UK	Bob O.	A R Panton & Sons, Ltd	Vitamin A	2120	60.0	135,300	30,086	22%	11,318	18,768	9,913	1,212	3,682	14,807	3,967	3%	32,808	12%
UK	Bob O.	Friends Soaps & Detergents	Color AZX	2210	150.0	215,250	89,122	41%	34,903	54,219	4,794	573	5,857	11,225	42,994	20%	27,363	157%
Germany	Joop K	Zusatz GmbH & Co KG	Color BEX	2210	30.0	22,386	3,818	17%	3,425	393	2,660	53	609	3,322	(2,929)	-13%	5,473	-54%
Germany	Joop K	Hahnemann GmbH	Stab 5310	3000	5.6	55,295	8,743	16%	11,856	(3,113)	23,216	155	1,505	24,876	(27,988)	-51%	10,124	-276%
Germany	Joop K	Hausser Werke	Premix EZ	4100	6.0	11,071	6,458	58%	2,360	4,098	3,793	724	301	4,818	(720)	-7%	3,280	-22%
Brazil	Antonio D.	Nao distribudor	Premix 25S	4200	1.1	74,022	42,290	57%	5,630	36,659	555	2,401	2,014	4,970	3,689	43%	8,115	390%
Poland	Joop K	Paradex s.c.	Premix 25S	4300	0.8	60,613	32,439	54%	4,504	27,935	710	1,904	1,649	4,263	23,672	39%	6,492	365%
USA	John A.	Food Production Corp	Citric Acid	5200	80.0	374,824	106,816	28%	37,288	69,527	17,625	25,720	10,200	53,545	15,983	4%	61,829	26%
USA	John A.	Duston Distributors	Citric Acid	5200	25.0	85,622	8,356	10%	8,965	(609)	12,356	1,982	2,330	16,668	(17,277)	-20%	19,222	-89%

Annotations:

R&D (research and development) projects and technical service are allocated based on:
– Business segment the project is for
– Customer the work is done for

G&A (general and administration) costs (including general management and accounting) are allocated proportionally to sales

S&D (sales and distribution) is a combination of:
– Sales costs
– Customer service desk
– Marketing and Advertising

FMC here denotes the costs of manufacturing and production

Note how misleading similar contribution margins can be. They often conceal large differences in true profitability (ROS and ROI)

Addit: Building trust from numbers

Susan Jones was well into developing her strategy when she realized something disturbing – her people didn't trust Addit's numbers.

In a regional meeting, this would play out something like this. The US marketing manager would declare that it didn't make sense to sell more of product A as it was unprofitable. He'd be fiercely countered by the manufacturing manager, who'd produce his own set of numbers. But his numbers would be dismissed by the marketing group. A discussion would ensue about how marketing was overstating its costs and manufacturing was understating their costs. The argument would then continue after the meeting through an e-mail exchange of numbers that all parties had acquired in their own way, and felt strongly were the right numbers. Needless to say there were no winners.

Sue determined to get the numbers straight – from the ground up. Addit needed one set of accurate and accepted numbers, she said, not just so they could make the right decisions, but also so that people could work together on a firm, factual basis.

The next weeks saw a flurry of activity. Each department was asked to review its full year costs and consider how these costs could be allocated to customers and products. A business analyst was hired to manage the data generated. Meetings were set up in which managers jointly decided how and why a cost should be allocated. Importantly, managers gained renewed insight. They were sharing more data, and gaining trust in each other.

The most substantive work took place on manufacturing costs, which comprised a large proportion of the total. These costs were not always straightforward to assign to one product or another. For example, how should one deal with salaries of plant staff such as the plant manager and the personnel department? But gradually, numbers were tallied, controls were run and corrections were made. When consensus was reached and the individual customer-product results were aggregated into business segments, the outcome was nothing short of astounding (Illustration 2.16).

What became clear was the wide spread of profitability. The numbers varied from a horrible loss of 22 per cent return on sales for new extracts to a huge profit, a return on sales of 30 per cent, for proprietary blends.

Some of these good returns, such as those from blends, were expected and in line with their contribution margins. However, other results – such as sweeteners – were a shock. For years, Addit had been supplying these materials to one of the largest users of sweeteners. Many in the company were proud of Addit's association with this customer. It was a jolt to see that despite a nice 51 per cent contribution margin, this area was Addit's largest loss-making business. It prompted angry debate before the numbers were finally accepted.

ILLUSTRATION 2.16

Addit's profit by segment

Code	Segment	Net sales (£m)	Contribution margin (£m)	CM%	Profit (£m)	ROS (%)
1000	**Animal nutrition**	**48,296**	**18,497**	**38%**	**3,480**	**7.2%**
1100	Pet food	13,717	4,895	36%	625	4.6%
1200	Pre-mixers	21,262	8,730	41%	2,562	12.0%
1300	Integrated manufacturers	13,318	4,871	37%	293	2.2%
2000	**Human nutrition**	**107,137**	**47,986**	**45%**	**10,334**	**9.6%**
2100	Vitamins	42,615	19,431	46%	8,433	19.8%
2110	*Food & beverages*	16,127	7,604	47%	3,395	21.1%
2120	*Supplements*	26,488	11,826	45%	5,038	19.0%
2200	Colors	30,362	12,765	42%	4,315	14.2%
2210	*Food*	14,132	5,998	42%	2,122	15.0%
2220	*Beverages*	10,965	4,536	41%	1,446	13.2%
2230	*Pharmaceuticals*	5,266	2,232	42%	748	14.2%
2300	Anti-oxidants	3,991	1,400	35%	(451)	–11.3%
2400	Sweeteners	18,811	9,614	51%	(1,403)	–7.5%
2500	New extracts	5,186	1,991	38%	(1,160)	–22.4%
2600	Other human nutrition	6,172	2,785	45%	599	9.7%
3000	**Personal care**	**25,588**	**6,622**	**26%**	**938**	**3.7%**
4000	**Nutritional blends**	**20,778**	**13,295**	**64%**	**4,188**	**20.2%**
4100	Proprietary blends	8,831	6,658	75%	2,674	30.3%
4200	Custom blends	5,076	3,259	64%	1,109	21.9%
4300	Standard blends	6,871	3,379	49%	404	5.9%
5000	**Other**	**75,062**	**27,508**	**37%**	**2,443**	**3.3%**
5100	Intermediates	22,144	10,590	48%	848	3.8%
5200	Plastic additives	11,713	2,917	25%	(233)	–2.0%
5300	Non-food citric acid	14,567	5,451	37%	1,324	9.1%
5400	Paint additives	5,992	910	15%	(471)	–7.9%
5500	Specialities	4,263	1,916	45%	(417)	–9.8%
5600	Distributors	16,383	5,724	35%	1,391	8.5%
Total		**276,861**	**113,909**	**41%**	**21,383**	**7.7%**

There were pleasant surprises too, especially in Addit's bread and butter business – vitamins. At almost 20 per cent ROS, this large business was very profitable and throwing off a lot of cash. This was extremely good news.

Vitamins had been regarded as unfashionable, even boring. Addit managers had been convinced the vitamins were barely profitable and so vital resources had been directed elsewhere. Realizing that as much as 39 per cent of Addit's profits were generated from this business, and close to 50 per cent from human nutrition as a whole, Sue gained a new perspective on what might be done.

SUMMARY

To summarize for your own business, determine the true profitability of your segments, either:

◆ Top down, by estimating how much more costly one segment is over another.

◆ Bottom-up, by assigning costs to each of your product-customer combinations, then rolling these up to the business segments.

Compiling segment profit data nearly always stands some perceived wisdom on its head and provokes thought about the direction of the business. When you run the numbers on your own business, you likely to find that some parts of the business are much more profitable than you thought before and some other 'good' business is in fact heavily loss-making.

It's wrong to jump to conclusions, however, before finishing the strategic diagnosis. Our next port of call is to get insight into how strong or weak each of our segments is in relation to our competitors.

4

....

HOW GOOD ARE YOUR COMPETITIVE POSITIONS?

You now want to find out how strong each of your business segments is in competitive terms, because strategy will differ accordingly. Assessing competitive strength is not as difficult as it sounds. Most of the insight available here can be gathered just by knowing four facts for each segment:

1. The business's relative market share (RMS) in the segment.

2. The trend in RMS.

3. The expected annual future growth rate of the segment's market.

4. The return on capital employed (ROCE) of each segment business.

Remember that the *relative market share* is the market share or sales that your firm has in the segment divided by the market share or sales of your largest competitor in the segment. Work this out now for each of your segments (again, you can use the software to get there quickly). If you are not exactly sure of your largest competitor's sales in the segment, make a note to find out later, but for the time being put down your best estimate. Now calculate the RMS. As an example, let's revisit Pasadena and the tea business.

Jack defines his relative market shares

After Jack's astonishment about his segment profitability (see Illustration 2.9), we spent the rest of Sunday morning with his marketing director, establishing how large UTC was compared with its competitors in the newly-defined segments. By noon we had the answers (Illustration 2.17).

ILLUSTRATION 2.17
Relative market shares (RMS) for UTC segments

Segment	UTC sales	Largest competitor	Competitor sales	UTC RMS
Branded Tea: US	$200m	United Foods	$150m	1.33x
Branded Tea: Canada	$23.7m	Canadian Tea	$25m	0.95x
Branded Tea: Europe	$45m	United Foods	$200m	0.22x
Branded Tea: ROW	$48.5m	United Foods	$15m	3.2x
Big Boy PL	$354m	Cheapco	$490m	0.72x
Small Fry PL	$36m	George's Contracts	$45m	0.8x
Herb Tea: US	$55.5m	Herbal Health	$20m	2.8x
Herb Tea: Exports	$11.0m	Auntie Dot's	$20m	0.55x
Fruit Tea: US	$23.2m	Fruit-Tea Fun	$8.5m	2.7x
FruitTea: Exports	$4.7m	Auntie Dot's	$10m	0.47x

How good are these relative market share (RMS) positions? First I explained to Jack and his marketing director some rules of thumb about them (see Illustration 2.18).

I then went on to tentatively classify UTC's segment position portfolio (Illustration 2.19). This looked, on the face of it, pretty good. But before coming to any judgements, I wanted to look at the *trend* in RMS.

ILLUSTRATION 2.18

Rules of thumb concerning relative market share (RMS) positions

RMS position	Name	Rule of thumb
4.0x or greater	Dominance	Extremely strong position
1.5x to 3.9x	Clear leadership	Very strong position
1.0x to 1.49x	Narrow leadership	Strong position
0.7x to 0.99x	Strong follower	Fairly strong position
0.3x to 0.69x	Follower	Moderate position
Less than 0.3x	Marginal player	Weak position

ILLUSTRATION 2.19

Strength of UTC segment positions

Segment category	Segments	Sales	% of sales
Dominance	–	–	0.0
Clear leadership	Branded Tea: ROW Herb Tea: US Fruit Tea: US	48.5 55.5 23.2	15.9
Narrow leadership	Branded Tea: US	200.1	25.0
Strong follower	Branded Tea: Canada Small Fry Retailers	23.7 35.9	7.4
Follower	Big Boy Supermarkets Herb Tea: Export Fruit Tea: Export	353.6 11.0 4.7	46.1
Marginal player	Branded Tea: Europe	45.0	5.6

This requires going through the estimates of RMS again (as in Illustration 2.17), but this time for the position in RMS as it was three years ago. Since then, have you gained or lost in terms of relative market share? The results for UTC's segments are shown in Illustration 2.20.

This looked like a deteriorating picture, although Jack's first reaction was that this was OK, since in the attractive export markets, the ones with the highest profitability, UTC was gaining share. I was not so optimistic, but before I could make any comments Jack had stood up to take another call.

ILLUSTRATION 2.20
Trend in RMS of UTC

Gaining share	Holding share	Losing share
Branded Tea: Canada	US Private Label	US Branded Tea
Branded Tea: Europe		US Herb Tea
Branded Tea: ROW		US Fruit Tea
Herb Tea: Exports		
Fruit Tea: Exports		
17% of sales	**48% of sales**	**35% of sales**

How does this picture compare to the trend in your segment positions? (If you enter your data using our software, it will generate the tables and displays here for you.)

Addit gets a taste of the market

To establish Addit's market position, we took it again from the bottom-up. For the main markets we asked the sales executives to report on sales of competitors to each of their customers. This worked excellently. In feed and vitamins Addit was so entrenched that the sales executives knew just about every customer, their total purchases and who else was supplying them. In other markets, estimates were taken from various executives and where they were different, looked at carefully. The exercise took just a few weeks to complete.

In the meantime, Addit's market growth was calculated.

Clearly, Addit has some strong positions (high RMS) in its key markets of animal and human nutrition, as well as in the blends. On the other hand there were some marginal positions, e.g. the segments number 5300 and 5500.

ILLUSTRATION 2.21

Addit RMS and growth data

Segment	Segment name	Addit sales (£m)	Largest competitor	Competitor's sales (£m)	RMS	Addit growth*	Market growth* Historic Growth	Market growth* Future Growth
1000	**Animal nutrition**							
1100	Pet food	13,717	Raben AG	4,876	2.8	4.0%	3.5%	3.5%
1200	Pre-mixers	21,262	BonGout	18,538	1.1	3.6%	3.6%	3.6%
1300	Integrated manufacturers	13,318	BonGout	11,564	1.2	3.5%	2.7%	2.7%
2000	**Human nutrition**							
2100	Vitamins							
2110	*Food & beverages*	16,127	Raben AG	4,705	3.4	3.5%	2.8%	4.0%
2120	*Supplements*	26,488	AdCorp	13,429	2.0	4.0%	3.5%	4.0%
2200	Colors							
2210	*Food*	14,132	BonGout	12,238	1.2	4.5%	4.1%	4.0%
2220	*Beverages*	10,965	Raben AG	2,872	3.8	4.0%	4.0%	4.0%
2230	*Pharmaceuticals*	5,266	AdCorp	2,726	1.9	4.0%	4.0%	4.0%
2300	Anti-oxidants	3,991	Cheapskills	10,545	0.4	1.5%	2.3%	2.0%
2400	Sweeteners	18,811	AdCorp	18,738	1.0	2.0%	6.0%	7.5%
2500	New extracts	5,186	AdCorp	40,000	0.1	15.0%	2.0%	4.0%
2600	Other human nutrition	6,172	Raben AG	37,926	0.2	2.0%	2.0%	2.0%
3000	**Personal care**	25,588	Raben AG	35,000	0.7	3.0%	3.5%	3.5%
4000	**Nutritional blends**							
4100	Proprietary blends	8,831	AdCorp	2,944	3.0	3.0%	2.7%	3.0%
4200	Custom blends	5,076	AdCorp	3,318	1.5	0.5%	0.5%	1.0%
4300	Standard blends	6,871	AdCorp	2,683	2.6	2.6%	2.6%	3.0%
5000	**Other**							
5100	Intermediates	22,144	AdCorp	21,000	1.1	1.7%	2.3%	3.0%
5200	Plastic additives	11,713	Bastion	112,500	0.1	1.1%	2.0%	3.0%
5300	Non-food citric acid	14,567	BonGout	102,000	0.1	2.0%	2.0%	2.0%
5400	Paint additives	5,992	Cheapskills	20,000	0.3	0.1%	2.0%	2.0%
5500	Specialities	4,263	Cheapskills	18,200	0.2	1.0%	2.0%	2.0%
5600	Distributors	16,383	AdCorp	5,345	3.1	5.0%	3.5%	4.0%

* After subtraction of inflation

Illustration 2.22 summarizes the strength of Addit's positions. This table takes into account both sales and profit in each segment category. As expected, Addit makes most of its profit in the segments where it has clear leadership.

ILLUSTRATION 2.22

Strength of Addit segment positions

Segment category		Segments	Sales (£m)	% of Sales	Profit (£m)	% of Profit
Dominance	> 4.0x	–	–		–	
Clear leadership	1.5–3.9x	1100 Pet food	13,717		625	
		2110 Food & beverages	16,127		3,395	
		2120 Supplements	26,488		5,038	
		2220 Beverages	10,965		1,446	
		2230 Pharmaceuticals	5,266		748	
		4100 Proprietary blends	8,831		2,674	
		4200 Custom blends	5,076		1,109	
		4300 Standard blends	6,871		404	
		5600 Distributors	16,383	40%	1,391	79%
Narrow leadership	1.0–1.5x	1200 Blends	21,262		2,562	
		1300 Integrated manufacturers	13,318		293	
		2210 Food	14,132		2,122	
		2400 Sweeteners	18,811		(1,403)	
		5100 Intermediates	22,144	32%	848	21%
Strong follower	0.7–1.0x	3000 Personal care	25,588	9%	938	4%
Follower	0.3–0.7x	2300 Anti-oxidants	3,991		(451)	
		5400 Paint additives	5,992	4%	(471)	–4%
Marginal player	< 0.3x	2500 New extracts	5,186		(1,160)	
		2600 Other human nutrition	6,172		599	
		5200 Plastic additives	11,713		(233)	
		5300 Non-food citric acid	14,567		1,324	
		5500 Specialities	4,263	15%	(417)	0%
Total			**276,861**		**21,383**	

The market growth data in Illustration 2.21 shows that with few exceptions Addit's market was mature and growing at the market rate or just a tad above. That information was used to determine the trend in Addit's RMS. For example, if the market had been growing faster than Addit's sales – as in the case of the Sweeteners segments – then in that area the RMS must have declined.

That's a bit of an easy way out. To be accurate, it would have been better to compare Addit's actual sales to the sales of the largest competitor, today and three years ago. Comparing those two RMS's would give a more precise picture. But this shortcut was allowed because Addit's marketing managers were sure that the relative positions for the big players had been stable. The results are shown in Illustration 2.23. Again, both sales and profits are compared in each category.

ILLUSTRATION 2.23

Trend in RMS of Addit

Improving RMS		Stable RMS		Declining RMS	
Code	Segment	Code	Segment	Code	Segment
1100	Pet food	1200	Blends	2300	Anti-oxidants
1300	Integrated manufacturers	2200	Beverages	2400	Sweeteners
2110	Food & beverages	2230	Pharmaceuticals	3000	Personal care
2120	Supplements	2600	Other human nutrition	5100	Intermediates
2210	Food	4200	Custom blends	5200	Plastic additives
2500	New extracts	4300	Standard blends	5400	Paint additives
4100	Proprietary blends	5300	Non-food citric acid	5500	Specialities
5600	Distributors				
	41% of sales		25% of sales		34% of sales
	67% of profit		38% of profit		–6% of profit

Armed with all the data, Sue called a full-day meeting with the strategy group to discuss the results. This was the first such gathering, and nobody knew quite what to expect. But once they started going through the tables, the managers loosened up. First they were very pleased to learn that Addit was occupying a good number of 'clear leadership' positions. These also made lots of money.

And as Illustration 2.23 shows, these were largely the same areas where RMS was improving or stable. More than 100 per cent of Addit's profit was generated by segments with improving or stable RMS. The business managers were starting to like this strategy thing!

Of course, there were also segments with falling RMS. When looking through them, one manager cunningly remarked that they shouldn't worry at all: 'We are making a loss there, so we already started to work on our exit strategy!' With so much good news, we sensed that perhaps the group was getting a bit too confident...

What about your market position? Calculate your segment strength and RMS trend tables (you can use our software to do this).

It's now time to introduce you to a new display, the GROWTH/GROWTH MATRIX (Illustration 2.24), which compares the growth in the market to the growth in your own business. We can superimpose bubbles (circles) to represent your segment businesses. By definition, where your businesses have grown faster than the market over the past few years, there will be bubbles below and to the right of the diagonal line (shown in Illustration 2.25 in black); where you have grown at exactly the market rate the bubbles will be centred on the diagonal line (shown as clear circles), and where your business has grown slower than the market, the circles (shown in grey) will be above and to the left of the diagonal.

Note that the size (area) of the circles is proportional to sales revenues (they can also be drawn with the area proportional to profits or to capital employed in the segments). We will use this convention throughout the book.

ILLUSTRATION 2.24
Growth/growth matrix

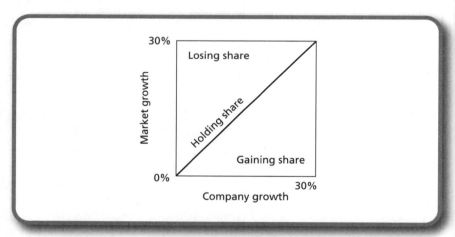

ILLUSTRATION 2.25

Growth/growth matrix with illustrative segment positions

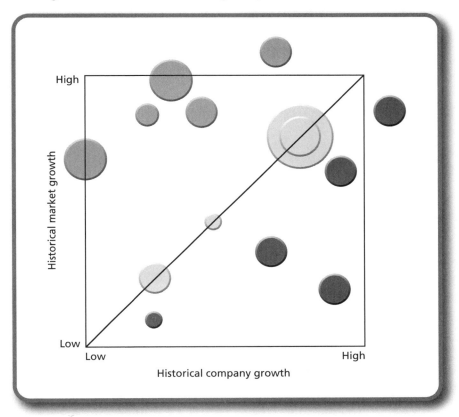

Jack looks at UTC's growth/growth bubbles

I thought that after lunch Jack and I, along with the marketing director, should mock up some charts showing the growth in the market and in their sales for the ten segments. After asking both of them a few questions, the chart generated looked like that in Illustration 2.26. Note that the size (area) of the circles is proportioned to the sales revenue. (The circles can also be drawn proportional to profits or capital employed in the segments.) Partly, Illustration 2.26 was just a graphic way of showing the information from Illustration 2.20, but it also showed an interesting pattern. First, there is about equal area in the circles to the left of the diagonal (where Jack was losing market share) and to the right (where he was gaining share). Also, note two other interesting facts.

ILLUSTRATION 2.26

UTC growth/growth bubbles

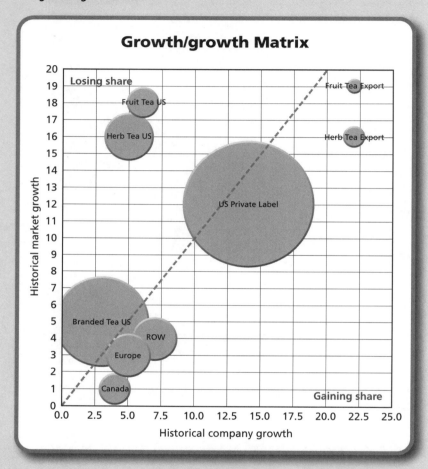

1. The markets for herb tea and fruit tea were both growing very fast every-where, at roughly the same rates (between 15 per cent and 20 per cent each year). Yet UTC's growth rate was very different, averaging 5 per cent in the US and more than 20 per cent in the export markets. This was because more marketing effort was going into the smaller export markets, in the mistaken belief that these were more profitable. In fact, UTC was losing market share in the profitable and high growth US markets. UTC was cutting itself off from most of the growth in the largest and most profitable segments: US herb and fruit teas. Surely Jack could do something about this!

2. The branded mainstream markets were low growth everywhere, while the private label market in the US was growing fast. This was bad news for UTC, because it made lower returns (in fact lost money overall) in the private label market. This trend explained why UTC's margins were sliding overall, despite growing sales. But it also raised the intriguing question of whether private label was growing in some of the export markets, and whether UTC could profitably enter any of these.

Before going further, we want to introduce you to three other charts on which to display your segment data. The first of these is perhaps the most famous strategic tool of all, the celebrated (and derided) GROWTH SHARE MATRIX. We do not need to be detained by a lengthy explanation of the theory behind it (those who are interested should consult the Glossary). All we need to know is how to use this matrix and how it helped UTC and Addit.

The growth/share matrix uses the dimension of market growth that we've just explained, except that you should plot your best estimate of the expected future annual market growth. Note that you should do this in terms of units of

ILLUSTRATION 2.27
Growth/share matrix

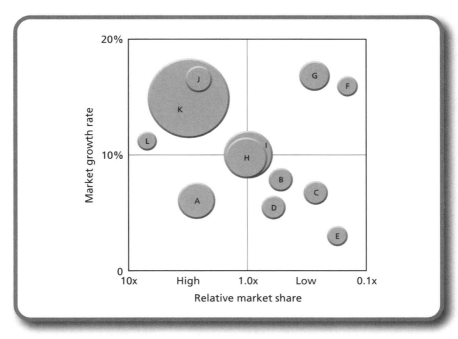

volume of the product or service. However, if you find volume more difficult to estimate than the value of the market in money terms, use value – but strip out inflation and take real value growth. The other dimension is relative market share (RMS). Now just go ahead and plot your segment positions on the matrix (see Illustration 2.27), again making the area of the circles correspond to your sales in each segment. (Our software will help you with all of this.)

Although many writers are sceptical about the growth/share matrix or regard it as old hat and discredited, our experience is that, when sensibly used, the matrix is a powerful diagnostic tool based on the real business segments we have discovered. The significance arises from the descriptions accorded to each of the quadrants of the matrix. First we need to give names to these (see Illustration 2.28).

ILLUSTRATION 2.28
Growth/share matrix quadrants named

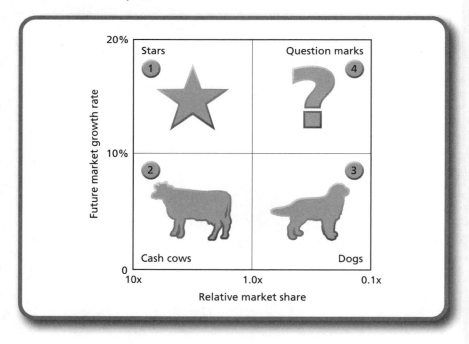

We will now give our own comments (adapted from the original Boston Consulting Group prescriptions) for the quadrants. Your job is to see if this gives you insight into any of your businesses.

The most interesting businesses and insight are in the top left, the STAR quadrant. Star businesses are where you are the market leader in a high growth business. Most of you will have few or no star businesses. For those of you who have them, realize first of all how valuable such a business is. If you manage to remain the segment leader, your profits from the segment should be very high and growing all the time. When the market growth cools off, you will have a large, valuable business that should still be very profitable and will begin to throw off very large amounts of cash (the bubble for this business will be in box two and will be a cash cow).

The rule for star businesses is to invest, invest and invest. Do whatever is necessary to hold, or if possible gain, market share. You will never regret doing so.

Box two contains the CASH COWS, business segments where you are the leader but where the growth is not particularly high. These businesses will generally comprise a minority of your sales, but a majority of your profits and cash generation. They are a classic illustration of the eighty-twenty principle: 20 per cent of the sales generating 80 per cent of the profits and cash (in fact, sometimes more than 100 per cent of the profits and cash). They are great businesses to have. The rule for cash cows is to make sure that they have the highest grade grass, that they are well protected, and that they grow even bigger and stronger.

Cash cows are generally quite easy to keep happy, since their appetites are nowhere near as voracious as those of stars. But remember – contented cows make bigger and better dollops of cash.

The bottom-right box, labelled three, is the DOG kennel. Forget all you have been told about dogs. They are a motley crew, but some of these businesses are valuable.

If they are towards the centre of the chart, that is, if they are towards the left of the box (although still on the right of the matrix), they are MARKET CHALLENGERS or strong followers, and likely to generate nice profits and cash. Try to gain segment leadership if this can be done without too high a cost. Otherwise look after these businesses well.

For businesses towards the right edge of the box, the really doggy dogs, not too much should be expected. Find out if any of them are losing money and are a cash drain. Sell these, and if you can't, close them.

Box four is in many ways the most intriguing, containing the QUESTION MARK businesses. They pose the greatest strategy dilemmas. On the one hand, it is nice to be in a high growth business, but on the other hand, it's bad news to have a weak market share position. If you could be confident about becoming the market leader (driving the business to the star position) this would be a great move. But this will cost you. And if you don't make it, you will never get your money back.

The answer with question marks is to be very selective. Only back those you know can become number one in the segment. Otherwise, think about selling the business if it is not too closely connected with your other businesses. You could get a very nice price (people always pay a lot for growth businesses, even those in weak competitive positions) and you won't risk pumping cash into a black hole.

Jack draws a growth/share matrix

Jack had liked his growth/growth bubble-chart, which was just as well, because he couldn't believe I was suggesting making a growth/share matrix. 'Jeez, Richard,' he said, 'never thought you would come with that. Thought that stuff was totally outdated.' I told him to trust me while I drew a blank growth/share matrix on a flip chart. 'The growth/share matrix is one of those tools that almost always gives useful insights. You want to get a strategy for your business, and this is a tried-and-tested way to get there.'

With only nine businesses to plot (he agreed to combine the two private label contracts) we did it fast. See Illustration 2.29. 'So what do you make of that?' Jack asked me, not bothering to hide his scepticism. Brushing that aside, I made five comments.

'First, that's a portfolio many managers would kill for. You have leadership in four segments and a lot of growth. Most portfolios are much weaker than this. So we ought to be able to find a way round the present difficulties.'

'Second, look at the US herb tea and US fruit tea businesses. The matrix says they are enormously valuable, but you haven't been treating them that way. If you carried on losing share they would drift over to the question mark box and end up as dogs. But it's probably not too late. You should be investing whatever it takes to hold share and even regain share in these two businesses.'

'Third, US branded tea at the bottom of the matrix. You're a leader, but not by a wide margin. And you're losing share, so this too could end up as a dog. You should probably aim to regain market share. But there's a question the matrix can't answer about whether this is a good business to be in. It's under attack and losing to private label. You think it's a bad business. I don't know. A final view on this will have to wait.'

'Fourth, herb tea exports and fruit tea exports are question marks. You're gaining share but still in very weak positions. We have to reach a view on whether you can gain leadership. That will have to wait until after we've studied competitors and talked to customers.'

ILLUSTRATION 2.29

UTC growth/share bubbles

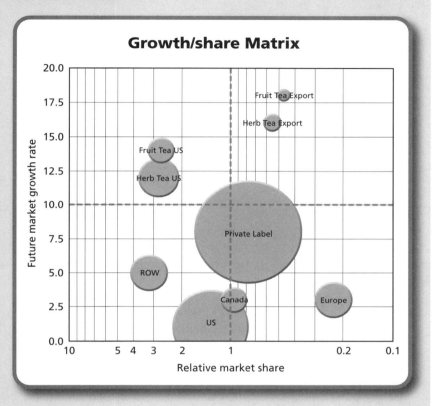

'Fifth, UTC has very different positions in branded tea in Europe, Canada and the rest of the world. Europe is very weak and not very profitable. Canada is fairly strong and has OK profits. Rest of the world is very strong and profitable. I'd try to consolidate even further here. I'd want to know how much it would take to become clear leader in Canada. On the face of it, Europe looks a lower priority unless we can think of something dramatic to do there.'

By the end of my monologue Jack was looking more thoughtful.

ILLUSTRATION 2.30
Draw our segments' RMS/ROS chart

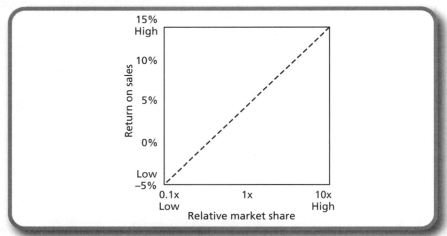

You may want to draw two other charts for your business as well. The first, called an RMS/ROS chart, simply displays the data on your segments' relative market shares and return on sales. As before, Illustration 2.30 is a blank chart on which to draw bubbles showing your segments' positions. (If you are using our software they will be generated automatically when you input the data.)

The reason this is interesting is that there is often, but not always, a positive relationship between high relative market share and high return on sales. If this does apply, it shows you the value of relative market share, and should reinforce your desire to increase RMS wherever possible.

But if there is no such pattern this, is also interesting. It may indicate opportunities or vulnerabilities for your business you'll see why if we return to Jack in Pasadena.

Jack gets the message from his RMS/ROS chart

After the insight from the growth/share matrix, Jack was alert and patient as I sketched out UTC's RMS/ROS chart (Illustration 2.31). He even turned off his cell phone and asked me what I made of it.

'Well,' I began, 'there is clearly a relationship: you tend to make the most money where you have the leading competitive positions. This should lead you to want to gain market share wherever possible, which we've just talked about. But the most fascinating thing is this big US private label blob, where the relative market share is not bad at all, but you're losing money.'

'Can't do anything about it,' Jack interjected. 'Cheapco can always undercut us. We've got higher overheads, what with marketing and all.' He shot a glance at the marketing director, who started looking uncomfortable.

ILLUSTRATION 2.31

Jack gets the message from the RMS/ROS chart for UTC

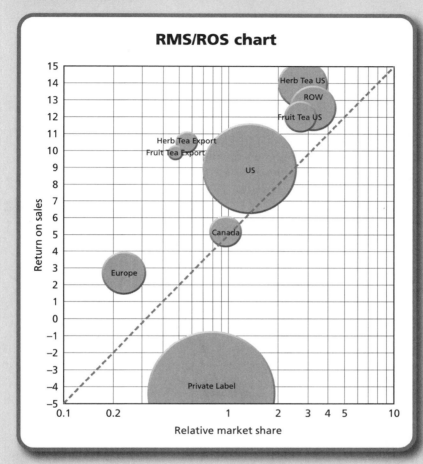

'We'll come to that later,' I retaliated. 'First I want to draw up the final chart, which will end this afternoon's session. It's very similar to this one, except it looks at return on investment or return on capital employed, instead of return on sales. The bottom axis of the chart remains relative market share, though I'm going to switch around the axes to keep you on your toes. In this chart (like the growth/share matrix) the best, highest, RMS positions are on the left. We call this chart the OPPORTUNITY/VULNERABILITY MATRIX, or Bananagram. You'll soon see why.' Then I sketched it out (Illustration 2.32).

ILLUSTRATION 2.32
Opportunity/vulnerability matrix for UTC

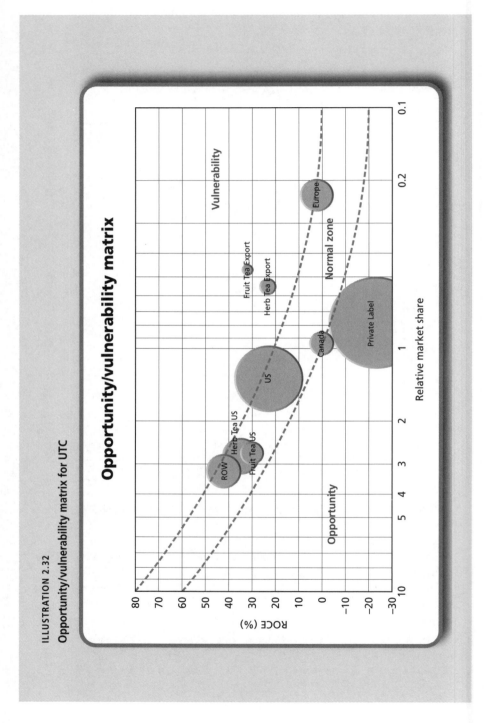

Opportunity/vulnerability matrix

Once I had drawn it, I took a marker pen and shaded in the band in the middle (marked Normal zone). 'This,' I asserted, 'is the Banana, more formally known as the normal zone or the normative curve. Experience and the collection of lots of boring data has shown that most business positions fall inside this band, because relative market share does correlate with profitability (in this case with return on capital). Roughly three quarters of all businesses I have looked at fall within this band, after proper segmentation and product line profitability. In a way this just shows the RMS/ROS relationship in another way. You got that Jack?'

He grunted, which I took as agreement. 'But of your nine positions, only five of them fall in the banana. The exceptions are worth looking at carefully. This chart says, first of all, that you may need to be worried about anything above and to the right of the band. We call this the vulnerability zone, because you have high profits without the high market share we would expect to back them up. The theory says that either these businesses must improve their relative market shares a lot, or you'd expect the profits to fall a lot.' I took a red marker and drew a circle around the two dots for exports of herb tea and fruit tea, and drew an arrow taking them down to the middle of the banana. 'The chart doesn't say that this will happen, just that it may.'

'But there's potential good news as well. Any business that is to the left and the bottom of the banana may be an opportunity. That business has high market share but low profits. And if you could take this private label business ...' I circled it in green, 'and take it up to the line,' I drew an arrow up, 'you'd make several million dollars more profit.'

'Can't be done,' Jack returned to his refrain. 'Maybe not, but maybe yes,' I replied. 'I haven't given up hope yet. The same applies in a much smaller way to the Canadian branded tea business – you may be able to improve its profitability a bit.'

'To do anything about these businesses, we need to look at them in much more detail, understand their economics, whether they are bad businesses, and know what the customers think about you and their other suppliers, your competitors. We need a bit more investigation for that, which I'll do next week, and we'll fix a time to meet again next weekend.'

'Good. Time to get back to work, guys,' Jack concluded. He looked much more cheerful now, though whether that was due to the news about his business or being able to go back to his e-mail, I couldn't tell.

Now that you have been fully introduced to the concepts of relative market share, the importance of market growth, and growth of your company through the different graphs, let's see how we used these ideas with Addit's managers to better understand that business.

Starting to like cows

After the initial cheerful reception, Sue and I proceeded to show the team the results using the different graphs.

First we looked at the key businesses of feed, the vitamins and colours used in foodstuffs, and the blends. Then we examined the problem areas, the segments where Addit had a weak position in the market, was losing share, or losing money.

Addit's key segments

Just as Richard did with Jack, Susan and I started with the growth/growth matrix to discuss the first set, Addit's key business segments (Illustration 2.33). For clarity, the two vitamin segments were combined into one bubble, as were the three colour segments.

ILLUSTRATION 2.33

Addit's growth/growth matrix for its business segments

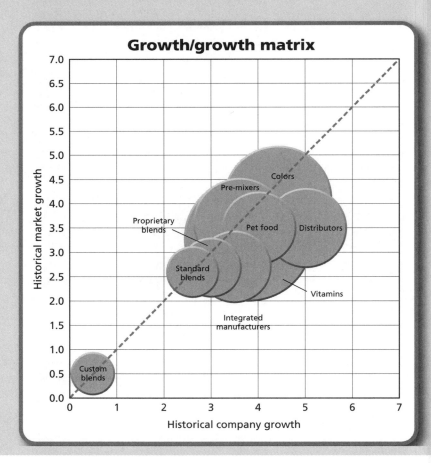

The graph confirmed what we had already read from the tables. Addit had been growing at or slightly faster than the market and so was slightly increasing its share. (You can see this quickly because there is more area to the right–bottom of the diagonal than to the left top.) Note that the scale is different from the UTC growth/growth graph due to lower market growth rates.

Next, the growth/share matrix of the segments shows that all are cash cows (Illustration 2.34). I explained to the group how very valuable these were. 'These are some great segments you have. Low market growth will prevent your competitors from building market share without you noticing. And if they

ILLUSTRATION 2.34

Addit's growth/share matrix for its business segments

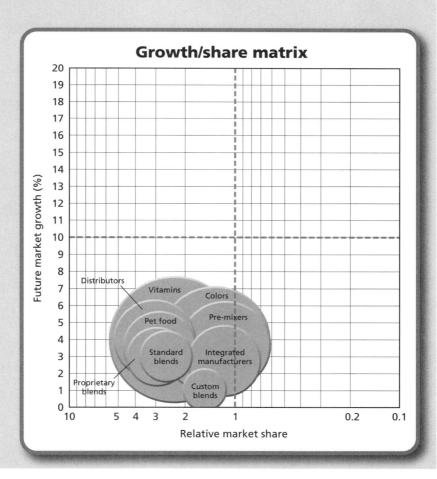

— 65 —

do try, you can ward them off because you are so much bigger than anybody else.' Under normal conditions, these cash cows would provide Addit with a secure stream of revenue for years to come.

The group was fascinated. Looking with them at these displays was like teaching a class of schoolchildren on a summer's day. Managers were visibly proud, congratulated each other, and some even questioned why we needed a strategy at all. How about 'business as usual'?

It was hard work to get them to focus on the most thought-provoking displays, the Bananagram (Illustration 2.35) and the RMS/ROS matrix (Illustration 2.36).

As I explained to the group, the bananagram shows that in many of its segments, Addit is making a better return than would be expected on the basis of its RMS. Only three of Addit's segments are inside the normal zone, while most segments are above, in the vulnerability area. The RMS/ROS graph backs up these findings, showing higher return on sales than would normally be expected from these relative market shares.

Now the executives were beaming. Surely these results had to be due to their superior business skills! Sue and I had to be very vocal to explain the mixed blessing of high-return market positions.

Of course, making above-average profits from your positions is great. And in some cases this is indeed the result of strong management or marketing. However, more generally such high returns are an indication of market inefficiencies – such as high entry barriers creating partial monopolies – which temporarily allow a whole industry to make more money. Addit's high returns may draw in new competition. Happy with lower prices and profits, such entrants would then bring the vulnerable segments down to more normal returns.

After all the good news, this message did not immediately hit home, although some team members started thinking about the implications. Addit had been acquired by its US owner largely for its stable cash flow. It was not a given that profits would fall, but the chart indicated that they could. The investors would be unpleasantly surprised if Addit's seemingly invincible cash cows faltered. The strategy would have to deal with this, not least to keep the management in place!

Worryingly, the bananagram and the RMS/ROS chart suggested that new entrants were already on their way. There are three segments with low ROS and ROI against RMS: distributors, pet food and the standard blends. For the distributor segment, the lower return is quite acceptable. These companies sell product on behalf of Addit. With lower costs in selling, Addit can offer sharp pricing to enable the distributors to make sufficient margin.

ILLUSTRATION 2.35
Bananagram for Addit's key segments

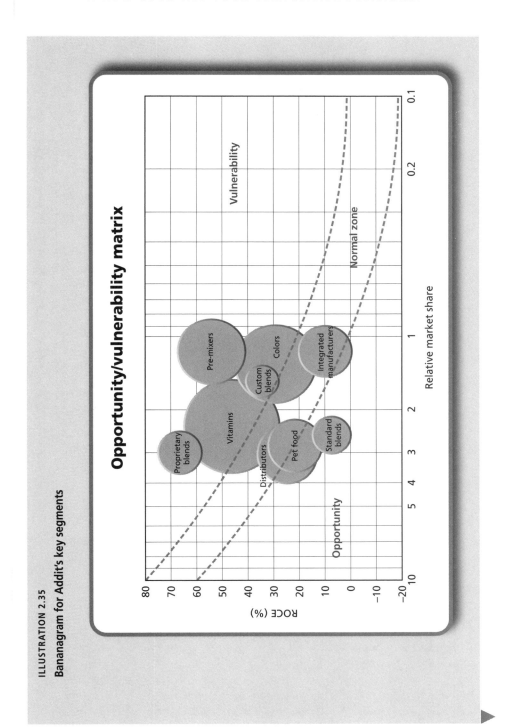

ILLUSTRATION 2.36
RMS/ROS chart for Addit's core segments

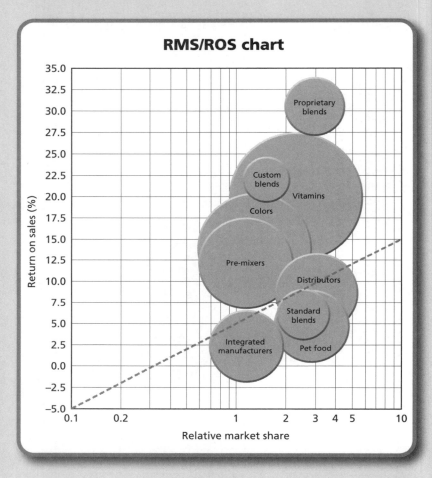

But why the lower returns in pet foods and standard blends? The team concluded that these were the result of price pressure from cheaper competitors. These competitors had only emerged in the past few years, but they were out in force, offering lower prices that Addit was having to match or approach. To maintain or improve profits here would probably mean that Addit would have to reduce costs.

Fortunately, so far the cheap competition was only active in Addit's less sophisticated segments. Other segments, such as vitamins and colours, required better quality products and compliance with legislation and standards on food and feed. But as Sue asked, 'What if the competitors' skills improve and they expand into segments like vitamins and colours?'

Some problems too

Once people had their feet on the ground again, attention turned to the additional, non-key segments that presented some additional challenges. Illustrations 2.37 and 2.38 show the growth/share and the bananagram of these areas. (The growth/growth and RMS/ROS diagrams can be found on *www.simplystrategy.com*).

ILLUSTRATION 2.37
Growth/share for Addit's other segments

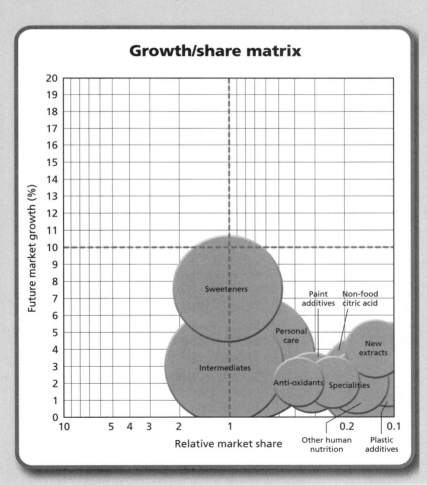

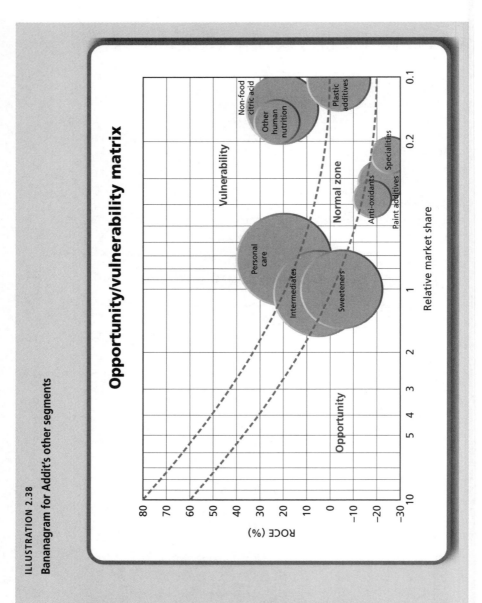

ILLUSTRATION 2.38
Bananagram for Addit's other segments

In all, ten segments, together representing almost £120 million in sales but a net loss, were examined. There was an opportunity here. 'Think about it. Right now Addit loses money on sales of £120 million. But if you could take this up to a mere 5 per cent ROS, you would make an additional £6 million profit.'

Would that be possible? The charts were giving us some good pointers.

The growth/growth matrix shows that Addit is losing share in each of these segments. The growth/share matrix (Illustration 2.37) shows that most of these segments are dogs, particularly in the 5000 ('other') area.

Sue asked the group for ideas to improve this. However, these 5000 sales were outside Addit's main expertise area and there was tough competition. Some managers admitted that defending these accounts was taking a lot of time and effort.

On the sweetener business there were some internal divisions to overcome. The new segment definition took into account Addit's share in the segment as a whole, not just the high share at one exclusive customer. That put Addit barely in a narrow lead in this segment. Worse, with the market growing 6 per cent, and Addit only 2 per cent (Illustration 2.21) Addit's position was getting worse.

This unleashed a torrent of questions and comments. Sue and I had to pull out all the data to convince the nay-sayers. The relevant managers found it all hard to swallow. They had made large investments and bet heavily on one customer. But as the data showed, that was not bringing the results they had hoped for. The customer was losing out to its competitors and Addit was being cut off from significant growth in the broader sweetener market .

Of course there was a solution – Addit could sell to other customers. At first, the team resisted that. Later, however, this move became a pillar of Addit's new strategy.

There was better news about new extracts. Sales in this segment – a dog in the growth/share matrix – were growing fast due to a product introduced four years ago. Addit was gaining share rapidly against its rival Adcorp, which would not have an equivalent product for some time. Consensus was reached quickly that the segment should be supported, to turn it into a cash cow by overtaking the Adcorp position.

Then we looked at personal care, another large segment. With competitor Raben in the lead, Addit here held a 'strong-follower' kind of dog position. This might have been OK, were it not that Addit was losing share. If nothing were done, this segment would only become more doggy. Sue asked the group what could be the cause of this, and was told that Raben had been getting ever more aggressive on pricing. Also, there was a new company, CheapSkills. The marketing managers indicated that often they could not match CheapSkills price, and had been walking away from some business.

While Addit was still doing well on its ROI in the area – largely because of written-off equipment – ROS was below expectations. Apparently Addit's costs were higher than Raben or CheapSkills.

Could the loss be reversed by introducing new, high return products? The idea was discussed but rejected. Over the past years personal care had become more and more about price. Customers didn't need the same high quality products as in segments like colour and vitamins, allowing less sophisticated players like CheapSkills to progress. Reluctantly, the group agreed that cost reductions would be the only way to arrest the slow share decrease and to keep profits up.

But once again Sue brought up her dreaded questions. What would happen if a CheapSkill-type competitor entered the food and feed area? What about the lower-cost players already eating into standard blends and pet food? But it was getting late. Before anyone could start a discussion, I put up a sheet with the conclusions for the day:

1. Addit is doing good business in its core segments of feed, food and blends. However, profits may come under pressure if low-cost competitors find their way into these fairly sophisticated segments.

2. In certain areas – notably standard blends and pet food – returns have fallen due to cheap competition. This suggests Addit's costs are too high.

3. Outside the core areas the results are mixed but again suggest high cost for Addit. These sales take a lot of time and effort that may be better deployed in higher return segments.

4. The sweetener area is Addit's only segment with high market growth, but it has been losing money and share. Addit needs to expand this segment through additional sales to new customers.

The team left for dinner with a lot to think about.

SUMMARY

Now that you have seen how UTC and Addit used the different graphs, take your time to discuss your graphs with your team. Answer at least the following questions:

◆ Growth/growth: Have you been keeping up with the market's growth?

◆ Growth/share: Have you been treating your business segments according to the quadrants that they are in? What strategic hints does the growth/share matrix give for your segments?

◆ RMS/ROS: Look carefully at those segments in which the ROS does not correlate with your RMS, whether positively or negatively.

◆ Bananagram: Which segments are opportunities (below the normality zone) and what would you need to do to improve? What is the cause for the segments that are vulnerabilities, and how can you prevent – or at least prepare for – your returns falling?

We've taken a long time exploring your competitive positions, but we hope you've found it rewarding. Segmentation, profitability, and relative market share are all related and looking at these three together is the fastest way to generate insight about a business. But now we need to understand what lies behind the strength in competitive positions.

5

WHAT SKILLS AND CAPABILITIES UNDERPIN YOUR SUCCESS?

Competitive positions should not be thought of independently of the skills and capabilities that make them possible. Where you are in leading positions, or gaining share, there must be a reason. Customers like what you have to offer, certainly, but why? Or, if you know that you are more profitable than other competitors, why is this? How can you make good money and yet also have delighted customers?

A question of skills for UTC

When I asked Jack this question, he was pretty dismissive. I had come to see him on a Tuesday morning, and his office was in full swing. Jack was going to meet with an important UTC supplier, the Big Boy contract was up for review, and one of Jack's plants would be proposing a machine upgrade. I could barely get two hours from him to think about the grounds of his success. 'It's because we've got good products,' he told me right off. 'Or,' he added after a brief pause, 'it's because we can make them cheaper and price them cheaper than anyone else.'

'Sure,' I replied, 'but why is that? How come? Why can you make something better and cheaper than any of your competitors? What's so special about your company and employees?'

I wasn't about to mention the jargon phrase CORE COMPETENCY, to Jack. That would just turn him off our discussion. I had no intention of saying that, way back in 1955, Philip Selznick coined the phrase 'distinctive competence' to mean what a firm was peculiarly good at. Nor was I going to refer to the hugely popular article in the *Harvard Business Review* of May–June 1990 by C.K. Prahalad and Gary Hamel called 'The Core Competence of the Corporation': the HBR would never make it into Jack's reading material. But I had the idea firmly in mind.

Jack was taken aback. I had to amplify, but tried to keep it snappy. 'Look: it's great to have good competitive positions, but you've got to ask what skills UTC has that have led to those good positions. What skills and resources, abilities and assets, what know-how, technology or other capabilities does UTC have, that give it leadership in branded tea and in herb and fruit teas in North America? What is it about UTC that customers like? How rare are these skills? Can competitors imitate them? How does the organization nurture these skills? And are the skills different across the different business areas? If you can't answer these questions, you don't know how secure your competitive positions are, how long they're going to last, or which business areas to consider entering.'

'Whoa,' complained Jack, 'that's a lot to ask! I thought I was going to get some real work done today.' I shook my head, part in disbelief, part to make him understand the reality and importance of this part of his job.

'You're basically asking what we're good at,' he started again. I nodded. 'Well, the first thing, I guess, is the brand. It's not really the supermarkets that love the brand, they'd rather flog their own house brands where they make more money. No, it's the end consumers. They just love our brands. Some consumers just won't buy anything else. And why's that? Beats me. It's part of American history the marketing people tell me, deep in the consumer's subconscious. And our brand also means very high quality. We've always been very focused on quality. Everything – the leaf tea we buy in, the way we process it, the packaging itself, to the product that stands on the shelves – it all has to be 100 per cent. If we find a damaged carton, a damaged box, we don't let it stay in the warehouse or on the shelves. Everyone is committed to quality, and what they call the integrity of the brand. It's very serious. Quality and the brand come first. We won't even change the advertising.'

'Is that true equally for all branded products?'

'Yep,' Jack replied confidently. 'The brands, the quality, they're equally critical for all the branded products.'

'But not the private label teas?'

'Not really. Well, obviously not, that brand isn't ours. Yes, we do still make a high quality product. Perhaps too much so. But the truth is, we don't really care as much about the private label teas.'

'And what about fruit teas and herb teas?'

'Same thing. The brand. It's just as important as in our regular branded tea. And, I guess, new flavours and new ideas are important too. We're good at that. Our R&D is the envy of the trade. Those guys are fantastic.'

'And what about my second question?' I asked. 'How rare are your skills in branding, quality, and product innovation?'

'Fairly. No, very. Nobody in our market is as good. Objective outsiders say so, even competitors admit it.'

'Why can't your competitors imitate you? What's stopping them filching your best market and R&D people? Why can't they develop skills as good as yours, perhaps not overnight, but after a while?'

'Hmmm. I'm not sure. Part of it is attitude. They haven't really tried. But you make a good point. I should make sure that we keep our best people, and that the attitudes are reinforced throughout the firm. I can see that it is important that we learn and deepen our unique skills, so that our success doesn't just depend on a few people, but rather is part and parcel of how we do business. I've always thought that was important. We need to do more to protect our key skills. Now, did you have any more questions on this tack?'

'No, you've pretty much answered the questions. When we come to consider new products, presumably we'll look for areas that can leverage and reinforce the strengths your company has: the brand, high quality, creative new product development?'

'Yep,' Jack concluded. His phone rang. His secretary walked in with a wad of papers to be read and signed. I decided to quit while I was ahead.

Ask yourself the same questions I asked Jack:

◆ *What is your business particularly good at doing? What is it that the customers really value? What skills and other assets underpin this success?*

◆ *How rare are these competencies in your industry?*

◆ *How safe are you from competitors imitating them? How can you make this more difficult?*

◆ *How can you deepen and reinforce the competencies throughout the business unit?*

◆ *Are the competencies different across the different business segments? Where are they most valuable?*

◆ *If you wanted to expand into adjacent segments, where would the competencies be most valuable to customers and least subject to imitation by competitors?*

When you work with a larger team to develop strategy, try the following approach, which usually works well. Take the inputs from a few experts and then broaden out so that the whole team can review and sign off the final results.

You probably want to involve between two and four managers, selected from different business regions, and veterans or experts in the business. With this group:

1. Establish between twenty-five and fifty of what we call the business' *skills*. These are business-specific capabilities that the business 'knows how to do', and which – importantly – are supported by the company's assets and resources. For example, a typical capability for UTC would be: 'We know how to find and purchase the best quality leaf tea.'

2. Identify among these capabilities between five and twenty so-called *distinctive skills*. These are the skills that make you as a business stand out in the market, and cause customers to choose you over other suppliers. For UTC the answer might be: 'We know how to introduce and sell innovative teas in the market.' This distinctive skill is supported by UTC's unique R&D assets and the strong collaboration between R&D and sales people.

These first two steps are depicted in Illustration 2.39. Once these steps are completed, a representative of the strategy group can review the results and approve them.

3. In a third step, get your people to narrow the skills down to three to five *competencies*. A competency is a combination of plain and distinctive skills that is more valuable than the sum of the parts. While skills are defined as specific as possible – to capture the essence of what the business is good at – a competency is defined as broadly as possible. The idea is to push its value to its maximum potency without becoming bloated, meaningless, or self-congratulatory (the latter is generally hardest!). For example, a number of skills in package design, the flavouring of tea, and bringing new teas to the market would combine as 'Development and marketing of innovative teas'.

To finish, the strategy representative once again reviews and possibly rephrases the competencies, and then presents the final version of the competencies, with the skills, to the strategy group. Usually, they agree, with minor changes and additions.

This approach is quick and efficient. Skills and competencies can be drawn up in two half-day sessions each. We've found that the quality of the results is independent of the number of people involved. Involving more people generally only adds time. You also need two review sessions of about two hours.

The biggest caution is that many businesses tend to think too much of themselves, listing capabilities that are run-of-the-mill or blatantly obvious and constructing competencies that they cannot support. Some experienced, down-to-earth facilitation goes a long way here to help arrive at good results.

ILLUSTRATION 2.39

Defining competencies in three steps

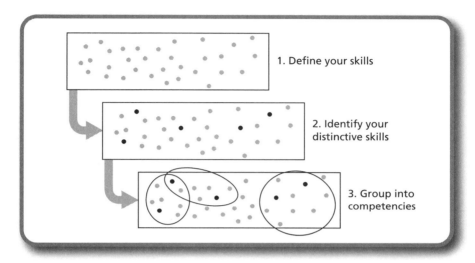

1. Define your skills

2. Identify your distinctive skills

3. Group into competencies

An exercise in modesty

I began the competency assignment at Addit with mild apprehension. Addit was a great business to work with, but its employees seemed just a bit too proud of their company's abilities. In fact, I thought this pride might be the reason for some of Addit's failings. I feared that drawing up 'core competencies' (as the managers persistently called it) would just be an open invitation for backslapping and self-congratulation. Anyway, whatever I thought, the job needed to be done. I had my first session with three managers, two of them old-timers and one recently hired. I would have no shortage of input.

After the introduction and objective setting, I started to list the skills that the managers brought up. Generally the strongest skills are mentioned first, and once the input dries up, I have my list of attention areas to be sure none are missed. But there was no need for that. Skills kept coming, and it seemed as if everything in Addit was top-of-the-bill – from manufacturing the products, to developing them, to how they were being shipped. I had to press on the brakes often, and hard. Again and again I asked the group: 'Isn't this obvious, commonplace? And if so, we shouldn't include it here, should we?'

For example, 'Addit knows how to safely ship products to customers across the globe'. But is Addit the only company able to request the services of shipping companies?

And when they said 'Addit knows how to make money,' I had to explain that we were looking for the reasons *behind* the profits.

I did get some good, down-to-earth input from the newer manager. Still, he was struggling to get his points across. His list of limited yet robust skills did not sit well with the grandeur put forward by the two veterans.

Gradually a picture emerged – a respectable company, with distinct strengths in the production and application of additives. But also a company not that unique in its skills.

The list of skills was reviewed by Jake, Addit's global manufacturing manager. A man of few words, he approved it without much ado. The competency session took too long but eventually generated a realistic list of competencies.

What Jake presented to Sue and the rest of the strategy group was sobering. Sue liked it. 'Guys,' she said to the group, 'this is just great. I understand each of these skills, and I can see how they add up to these competencies. This is what we should run with.' I agreed, of course. But I also knew that many members had secretly hoped for a grander list of core competencies. It was all part of the strategy game. The group came to realize that it was better to describe Addit's strengths modestly and accurately:

1. *Regulated production of vitamins, colours and related additives.* This relates to Addit's *dependability* in production. The observance of government regulations and industry standards is integrated into Addit's way of working. The products are high quality, and customers can count on Addit to supply on time and with the correct products, allowing them to cut back on inventory. But a number of Addit's competitors are equally adept at this. Also Addit is not cheap (otherwise you would have seen 'cost-efficient production' as part of the competency), and that presents a problem in areas that are less regulated, such as personal care.

2. *Marketing and application support of food and feed additives in Europe and the US.* Addit has a strong field presence in the US and in Europe. Technical sales people have long-term relationships with customers and can be called upon for advice and support. But service in Asia is spotty, hence Addit did not use the word 'global' in this competency – a pointer for future strategy decisions.

3. *Additive know-how for food, feed and personal care.* Beyond a presence in the field, Addit also knows a lot about which additives to use for food, feed and personal care, and how to best use them. For example, certain additives are best added early in the beverage-making process, others at the end. Customers value this know-how. But some of the larger customers in the food and feed industry are equally good or better at this, and don't need Addit.

4. *Global marketing and technology of nutritional blends.* Addit's most distinctive competence is knowing how to make liquid blends, what should be added when, what cannot be part of the mix. It is a craft, drawing upon talent and experience, best compared with making sauces that you don't want to separate or have flour lumps in. Some customers tried to replicate it ('this is just mixing a few ingredients, isn't it?') but failed, ending up with lumps or pastes. Buying the blends from Addit turned out to be the time- and cost-effective solution.

Note what was *not* mentioned. There is no competency in the area of Sweeteners, a painful admission for a company once so proud of its activities in this area. Also, there is nothing on anti-oxidants. Although it has sizeable sales, Addit is a follower in this business, not just in market share, but also in terms of skills.

Altogether an exercise in modesty. Addit was no more or less successful a company than it was before the competency working sessions. But by looking each other deep in the eyes, managers had gained a new perspective, a better appreciation, connecting past successes and failures to new realities. They were getting ready for change.

SUMMARY

To recap, there are two ways to determine your competencies:

Either take the view of the chief executive, or another high level manager, like Richard did with Jack.

Or ask two or three well placed executives to determine the competencies using these three steps:

◆ Define the firm's skills, the things it 'knows how to do';

◆ Identify amongst these the distinctive skills; and

◆ Synthesize three to five competencies.

The outcome can then be presented to your strategy team to be signed off.

6

IS THIS A GOOD BUSINESS TO BE IN?

Competitive position and the competencies that underpin it are one thing – the attractiveness of an industry or market is something different again. One determines whether you win the race, the other how much the race is worth. There have been long and boring disputes about the relative importance of the two factors, but we need not bother with these. At the extreme, an industry where nobody makes money and never will is of no interest, and even a leadership position in this situation is worthless. Moreover, there are industries (albeit very few) where almost everyone makes very high returns, regardless of competitive position. Our experience is that industry attractiveness on average explains about 30 per cent of the difference in firms' profitability, and competitive position within the industry (including an individual firm's management skill and culture) about 70 per cent. That is why we started with competitive position of the segments. But industry attractiveness is unquestionably important.

A good industry or market will have the following characteristics:

◆ *High returns on capital for players accounting for most of the market.*

◆ *A stable or rising average industry return on capital.*

◆ *Clear barriers to entry, keeping out many new entrants.*

◆ *Capacity at or below the level of demand, and low exit barriers.*

◆ *Reasonable or high market growth.*

◆ *Little or no threat from substitutes (competing industries).*

◆ *Low bargaining power of suppliers relative to the industry.*

◆ *Low bargaining power of customers relative to the industry.*

Let's comment briefly on each of these.

The best empirical measure of industry attractiveness is the *return on capital* employed for the industry, weighted by sales. Not everyone has to earn a high return, but companies supplying the bulk of the market should have a high average, well above the cost of capital. Many cute theories about particular industries' attractiveness or lack thereof can be quickly disproved by looking at the weighted average returns on capital in them. Many professional service businesses, for example, are alleged to be fiercely competitive and unattractive, but you wouldn't know this if you looked at the returns. Similarly, people often disparage 'commodity' businesses, without realizing that many of these can be highly profitable.

The *trend in ROCE* is also important. If it is falling, from whatever level, this is often a warning signal. On the other hand, some industries invest very heavily at the outset but show steady increasing returns on capital as volume builds.

BARRIERS TO ENTRY include investment scale, branding, service, cost to switch, a lock on distribution channels or sources of raw material, property/location, expertise or access to highly skilled people, patents, ability to produce at low cost, corporate aggression towards newcomers, and secrecy. Each of these is discussed in the Glossary.

The industry *demand/supply balance* and *BARRIERS TO ENTRY* are also clearly important. Barriers to exit include costs of firing employees, investment write-offs, disengagement costs, costs shared with other parts of a business, customer requirements for a 'package' of goods and services and non-economic factors such as pride or desire to keep a large empire.

Market growth, especially the recent trend, shows how healthy demand currently is, and how well the industry is coping against competing products.

The *threat from substitutes* can arise from competing technologies (gas, electricity and nuclear power versus coal, or airlines versus railways), or simply from products that consumers tend over time to prefer (wine versus spirits, healthier versus less healthy foods, convenience versus labour-intensive products, green versus non-green products, etc). A threat from substitutes may exist and be very serious, but may not yet show up in the statistics, as was the case with the threat to paper-based organizers from electronic ones.

The *relative bargaining power* of the industry vis-à-vis its *suppliers* and *customers* is pivotal. Broadly speaking, if an industry has a more concentrated structure (fewer suppliers accounting for, say, 75 per cent of total output) than its suppliers or customers, it will tend to have greater bargaining power.

In the 1950s and 1960s, most grocery and fast-moving consumer goods manufacturers had more concentrated industries than either their suppliers or their customers (the retailers). Since then, they have generally maintained the advantage over suppliers, but in most countries the emergence of a few large supermarket chains has wiped out the manufacturers' advantage over the retailers. Both groups are now highly concentrated. Both still have high returns on capital, but that of retailers has gone up while that of most grocery manufacturers has stabilized, indicating that the advantages from greater industry efficiency have tended to go to the retailers rather than the manufacturers.

The relative power of suppliers includes that of individual employees. In some industries (notably entertainment and investment banking) the power of an individual star can redirect profits from corporations to individuals. The singer George Michael can take on Sony. Bond or foreign exchange traders can try to double their pay, or threaten to go down the road for a multi-million dollar golden hello. Over the next decades, we will see a redistribution of corporate super-profits in 'knowledge industries' from shareholders to the most highly valued employees.

Industry attractiveness, then, is a many-headed monster. One problem with such a long list of attributes is that it is difficult to provide an objective quantification – industry attractiveness is very much in the eye of the beholder. Talk to ten people in the same industry but in different firms, and you often get ten different opinions.

To reduce the subjective element, we have produced an *industry attractiveness checklist*, which you can now apply to your own business or businesses. If you have a very focused business, and are active in only one industry or business area, you can just go through the checklist once. However, it is more likely that your activities are spread over different industries – go through the checklist separately for each one.

Don't go overboard and check all of your segments. A segment is not normally an industry. If you have ten segments, it is likely that you will need between three and six groups for the purpose of assessing industry attractiveness.

SUMMARY

Industry attractiveness

1. What is the weighted average ROCE (Return on Capital Employed) in your industry over the past five years?

Score: whatever the average ROCE is, with minimum of 0 and up to a maximum of 40.

2. What is the trend in ROCE over the past five years?

Score: (a) falling – no points; (b) erratic and no trend – 3 points; (c) stable – 7 points; (d) rising – 10 points.

3. How substantial are the barriers stopping new entrants to the industry?

Score: (a) few barriers – no points; (b) low barriers – 3 points; (c) fairly high barriers – 7 points; (d) very high barriers – 10 points.

4. What is your best estimate of the next five years' average annual market growth?

Score: (a) negative – no points; (b) 0–5 per cent – 3 points; (c) 5–10 per cent – 7 points; (d) over 10 per cent – 10 points.

5. What is the current balance in the industry between customer demand and the total industry capacity?

    Score: (a) there is serious industry overcapacity and no plans to remove it – minus 20 points; (b) there is serious overcapacity, but plans are in place to remove the excess – minus 10 points; (c) there is minor excess capacity – minus 5 points; (d) supply is in line with demand, or lower than demand – no points.

6. What is the threat from substituting products, services or technologies?

    Score: (a) serious threat – minus 20 points; (b) may be a serious threat, but uncertain – minus 10 points; (c) only minor threats expected – minus 3 points; (d) threats do not appear to exist and unlikely – no points.

7. What relative bargaining power do the industry's suppliers have?

    Score: (a) the suppliers are more concentrated and can dictate terms to the industry – no points; (b) the suppliers are slightly more powerful and concentrated than the industry – 3 points; (b) the suppliers are slightly less powerful than the industry – 7 points; (d) the industry is more concentrated and more powerful than the suppliers and can dictate terms to them – 10 points.

8. What relative bargaining power do the industry's customers have?

    Score: (a) the customers are more concentrated and powerful – no points; (b) the customers are slightly more powerful than the industry – 7 points; (c) there is a rough balance between the power and concentration of customers and the industry – 12 points; (d) the industry is more concentrated than the customers and has more collective bargaining power because there are few suppliers and little choice – 20 points.

Interpreting the scores

The scores will range between minus 40 and plus 100. Industry attractiveness can be interpreted as follows:

Negative score (minus 1 to minus 40): try to get out of the industry. If you are still reporting profits or anyone is foolish enough to buy the business, sell.

Score of 0 to 25: this is an unattractive industry. If you are not the market leader, sell the business.

Score of 26 to 50: the industry is not very attractive, but it is possible for segment leaders and very well run firms to make a living.

Score of 51 to 60: the industry is neither attractive nor unattractive. Competitive position is all.

Score of 61 to 75: the industry is attractive. If you are in it, consolidate your position and gain or maintain leadership. If not, consider entry if it is adjacent to your business and you have the expertise or can share costs with your existing business.

Score of over 75: the industry is unusually attractive. If you are in it, invest heavily for leadership. If you are not in it, you may find it difficult to enter without acquisition, but if there is a suitable way in, take it with both hands.

In this checklist, the contribution of the average ROCE score to the total score is significant, and warrants careful attention. Industry-wide ROCE is also not all that straightforward to establish. Probably you will want to construct a simple model that looks at the three or four main players, taking into account relative product pricing, costs and the size and history of their investments. Some market research may also do the trick.

Richard helps Jack to test industry attractiveness

The week after I saw Jack, I was busy on other assignments. But I did ask an assistant at UTC to check the ROCE for firms in the tea business, both branded suppliers and firms such as Cheapco that manufacture just for retailers' own labels. The following weekend, armed with my industry attractiveness checklist and these data, I returned to Pasadena.

Jack rapidly agreed that we should do the checklist separately for his branded and unbranded tea businesses. 'That's what you persuaded me of last time: unbranded stinks!' he said emphatically. He was therefore surprised to find that Cheapco and the other unbranded specialists had an average ROCE of 20 per cent, exactly the same as the average for the branded suppliers. He found that difficult to reconcile with his heavy losses in the unbranded segment. Still, he knew that barriers to entry were lower without a brand, and so was confident that unbranded would turn out to be a bad business. He wasn't sure that branded tea manufacture would score very well either.

When we went through the test, there were surprises for Jack. Not only was the unbranded tea ROCE as high as branded tea, but it was also rising over time, whereas the branded tea average was stable. Branded scored higher on barriers to entry, but lower on market growth. And when we came to the last question, we realized that whereas the degree of concentration and power was roughly the same for branded tea manufacturers and the retailers, the latter actually had less choice when it came to unbranded suppliers. There were very few of these, since the manufacturing scale required was a barrier to most firms and none of the branded manufacturers apart from UTC would supply private label as a matter of policy.

The scores are shown in Illustration 2.40.

As you can imagine, I had to battle to keep Jack's prejudices in check. When he had finally accepted the scores, he restated his puzzlement: 'If unbranded tea supply is very attractive, how come I lose money in it?'

'I don't know,' I replied. 'But Cheapco must be doing things differently. Perhaps they get a higher price than you do. Almost certainly they have lower costs. But if you did what they do, you could get costs as low. What we have realized is that the retailers are not as much in the driving seat as we thought.

ILLUSTRATION 2.40

UTC's industry attractiveness scores

Test		Branded tea		Unbranded tea	
		Result	Score	Result	Score
1.	Industry ROCE average	20%	20	20%	20
2.	Trend in ROCE	(c)	7	(d)	10
3.	Barriers to entry	(d)	10	(c)	7
4.	Future market growth	(b)	3	(d)	10
5.	Capacity/demand balance	(d)	0	(d)	0
6.	Threat from substitutes	(c)	−3	(c)	−3
7.	Suppliers' power	(d)	10	(d)	10
8.	Customers' power	(c)	12	(d)	20
Total score			59		74
Verdict		Attractive		Unusually attractive	

It's time to talk to them, the customers and to look more closely at the competitors, especially Cheapco.'

'And another thing,' I added, 'cheer up, Jack. Your branded business is attractive too. And your segment competitive positions are not at all bad on average. So we should be able to find a way to make more money for you, so you can keep your job and keep buying me lunch.' He was slow to take the hint, but eventually he took me out to a cheap coffee shop nearby.

At this point we would like to introduce you to a matrix that will be helpful in interpreting your industry attractiveness. This is the BUSINESS ATTRACTIVENESS Matrix (or BAM) – see Illustration 2.41. It has the familiar sales bubbles plotted according to their industry attractiveness score and relative market share (RMS).

Some people prefer to plot industry attractiveness against the more subjective measure of 'business strength' instead of RMS. Their criticism is that RMS does not take into account factors like brand strength, cost position or technological expertise, which they want to rate separately. This can be useful when a company has only recently entered an industry, and the RMS does not yet reflect your true strength. But otherwise it is just an invitation for a lot of debate. In the long run and in established industries, RMS is always the most reliable and objective measure of business strength. It's how the customer votes.

The matrix is divided into nine quadrants, each with its own implication concerning the attractiveness of your businesses. Like the growth/share matrix, it helps you decide where to deploy scarce resources, such as cash, know-how and employees.

In this case, the most obviously attractive businesses for investment would be D, followed by G and then probably C or F. Just like the question mark segment in the growth/share matrix, Business C could be a very good investment target, but only if the investment could drive it to a very strong position in the market (i.e. move it from the top left to the top right). If this does not seem likely, it may be best to sell C if a high price can be obtained. Businesses A and B are also disposal candidates at decent prices.

The business attractiveness matrix complements the growth/share matrix. The BAM is useful because – through the industry attractiveness score – it takes into account several factors about the industry/market.

ILLUSTRATION 2.41
Business attractiveness matrix (BAM), bubble size by sales

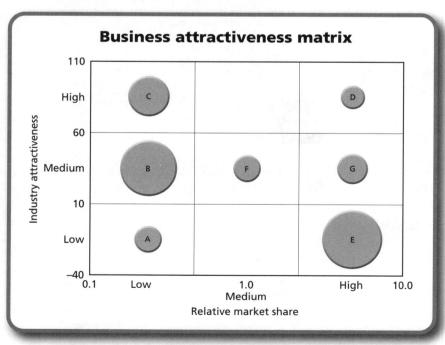

For any company it is useful to position all businesses on both matrices, and see whether the prescribed recommendations are different. If they are, carefully examine the assumptions leading to the difference.

To construct your business attractiveness matrix, choose the groupings of segments for which you want to determine industry attractiveness and then fill out the industry attractiveness checklist, manually or using our software. Adding the RMS will then generate the matrix for your company.

Good news for Addit

Sue and I charged a group of four executives with the task of determining industry attractiveness. They would focus on Addit's main businesses (in order of importance, and combining segments in 'industries'): vitamins, colours, blends, animal nutrition, personal care, sweeteners, and anti-oxidants.

The group would also make estimates about the larger segments in the 'Other' area, relying on outside market research.

The work consisted mainly of internal interviews and took six weeks to complete. The team constructed a financial model to estimate competitors' ROCE. From that they derived the weighted average ROCE. The scores and verdicts for the industries are summarized in Illustration 2.42. (Go to *www. simplystrategy.com* if you want to check the individual tallies.)

As usual, the scores and underlying details were discussed at a meeting with the strategy group. This time, the results were accepted with little discussion and some constructive dialogue ensued as to what these results would mean for Addit's strategy.

Illustration 2.42 shows that Addit's businesses score across the range from unattractive to attractive. Encouragingly, Addit's heartland businesses of feed (animal nutrition) and vitamins came out well, both being attractive. This was due to high and stable returns on capital, combined with fairly high entry barriers and a balance of power between customers and the industry. Happily, the sweetener business scored well too, the result of higher growth and rising profitability. This gave some consolation to those managers who had been depressed by this segment's bad financial results.

Of all Addit's main positions, personal care was faring the worst with lower and falling return, low entry barriers and less bargaining power than customers. This industry's poor attractiveness score corroborated Addit's weak financial returns.

With 45 and 48 points respectively, the colours and anti-oxidant industries were poised between personal care and vitamins. This was not so much due to lower returns in the colour business, but more because of lower entry barriers and increased bargaining power of customers.

The blends industry obtained a 'competitive' verdict, which was a surprise given the very good financial returns provided by this business. Also Addit had

ILLUSTRATION 2.42

Addit's industry attractiveness scores and verdicts

Code	Segment	Sales (£m)	Industry Attractiveness Score	Verdict
1000	**Animal nutrition**	**48,296**	61	Attractive
2000	**Human nutrition**	**107,137**		
2100	Vitamins	42,615	64	Attractive
2200	Colors	30,362	45	Not very attractive
2300	Anti-oxidants	3,991	48	Not very attractive
2400	Sweeteners	18,811	64	Attractive
2500	New extracts	5,186	63	Attractive
2600	Other human nutrition	6,172	n.a.	
3000	**Personal care**	**25,588**	33	Not very attractive
4000	**Nutritional blends**	**20,778**	57	Competitive
5000	**Other**	**75,062**		
5100	Intermediates	22,144	23	Unattractive
5200	Plastic additives	11,713	61	Attractive
5300	Non-food citric acid	14,567	38	Not very attractive
5400	Paint additives	5,992	57	Competitive
5500	Specialities	4,263	n.a.	–
5600	Distributors	16,383	n.a.	–

a close-to-monopoly market status, indicating high barriers to entry and low bargaining power for customers. However, upon closer analysis of the blends industry, only the proprietary blends segment was very attractive (on its own it could have been classified as an 'unusually attractive' industry). With the custom and standard blends mixed in, the blends industry as such scored lower on the average. This sent a warning to Addit not to stake too much of its future on the Blends. It is low-growth, a bit of a niche and, with the exception of the proprietary segment, not all that attractive.

The 'other' businesses constituted a mixed bunch, with intermediates very unattractive, while the plastic additives came out positively. Finally, the extract industry scored well, driven by good returns and low customer bargaining power. This lent support to the earlier decision to enter this area.

Following this analysis, we showed a plot of Addit's industries as a business attractiveness matrix (Illustration 2.43). The familiar bubbles represent Addit's sales volume, and they are plotted against their industry attractiveness score, and Addit's relative market share.

ILLUSTRATION 2.43

Business attractiveness matrix for Additt

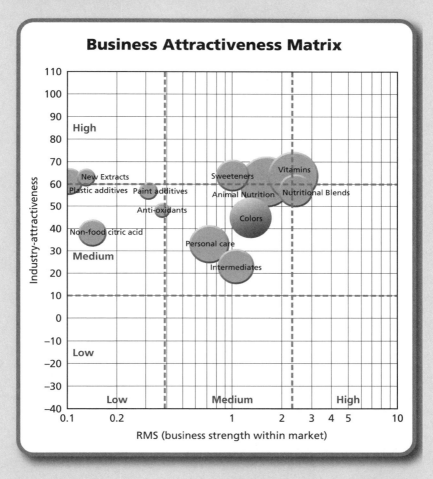

The plot served two purposes. First, it allowed the group to prioritize its cash cows, of which Addit had quite a few. Secondly, we discussed those positions for which the growth/share matrix and BAM lead to different conclusions. Let's go through both.

The group quickly decided that the main areas for future investments and management attention should be vitamins, blends, and animal nutrition (feed). Each of these businesses was a cash cow, but the BAM clearly prioritizes them over other cash cows, notably colours.

Next, the team agreed that more attention to the sweeteners business was warranted. A few team members argued that Addit's RMS was not a proper measure of its business strength. Due to its dedication to just one customer, Addit's RMS was lower than it could be, if you took other aspects into account – technology, experience, brand. Others countered that a one-customer supply situation is just not the same as a portfolio of customers and hence that the RMS was a good or perhaps even inflated measure of Addit's strength. Whatever the interpretation, all agreed that the sweetener industry was just as attractive as vitamins and feed. It would be justified for Addit to aim to improve RMS in the coming years.

While less attractive than vitamins, Addit's main businesses in the middle quadrant, colours and personal care, deserve attention. Their market shares had to be maintained and cost reductions were probably needed. Their industry attractiveness rating, however, indicated that they were not the top priority for investment.

While everyone agreed with the findings and conclusions for these segments, the positions of anti-oxidants and non-food citric acid caused considerable debate. There was no discrepancy between the growth/share matrix (which shows both these segment as dogs) and the BAM ('not very attractive'). The real issue was the industry attractiveness verdict: 'It is possible for segment leaders and very well run firms to make a living'. But Addit could not hope to become the leader in non-food citric acid and was losing more than 10 per cent on sales of anti-oxidants.

This meant that Addit should consider sale or exit. This disconcerted quite a few managers. They said that the segment was an important complement to Addit's core food business. And non-food citric acid shared production assets with other food and feed sales. Should one sell a business that makes decent money? Or one with sizeable sales in a core business area?

Sue listened and then calmed everyone down. 'I understand your questions,' she said. 'But if you think about it, the argument can also be reversed. Who wants to pay a good price for a loss-making or trivial-size business? So, making a profit or having a good position are not disqualifications for selling a business.' The group got that point quickly. 'Really all that should matter to us is what we can do with our time and money in these segments *compared with* spending that time and money in others.' She asked the group: 'Do you think that these segments will be a source of long-term profits for Addit?'

Some managers said they thought so, but most were doubtful. Extra effort would certainly be needed. Maybe an acquisition to boost share? 'Possibly,' replied Sue 'but since we can only spend our money and effort once, should we not spend it in areas where we are most certain of a good return?'

The main issue was Addit's limited experience with selling (or buying) parts of its business. Managers struggled with what that would mean in practice Would employees be fired? Would managers see their jobs diminished? But as Sue explained, selling part of a business can lead to more Addit, not less. 'Suppose, just suppose we would sell non-food citric acid,' she said. 'That's £14.5 million revenues and we could get anywhere between £8 and £13 million. We can return that to our owners, but I think they rather want us to re-invest in a business that generates higher returns.' The group started to see some new possibilities.

Lastly the team looked at businesses that came out differently in the BAM compared with the growth/share matrix. There were four and they could be quickly agreed upon:

1. Sweeteners. This business is borderline cash cow but attractive in the BAM. Addit's team had already decided they should increase their efforts here.

2. Intermediates. Another business that is borderline cash cow. But the BAM classifies it as an unattractive industry, suggesting Addit should not put a lot of effort here but rather harvest what value is available.

3. New extracts. This is a doggy dog in the growth/share matrix, because Addit had only just entered it. But its high attractiveness in the BAM justifies that decision. Both matrices added urgency to lifting sales and market share, to get a payback for the investments.

4. Plastic additives. A doggy dog business, but scoring (borderline) attractive as an industry. This is the best 'other' industry Addit has. But some argued that Addit would be out of its depth in this area and up against some very experienced and large competitors. It would be a long shot to become a prominent player in this segment.

Sue summed up:

'I think industry attractiveness shows once again we hold a nice hand of businesses, especially in food and feed. We should count our blessings because not every business is so fortunate.' The group smiled. 'But the analysis also tells us more about the why. So far, the barriers of entry into our feed and vitamins industry are high enough. But until some time ago they were also high enough in personal care, and we all know what happened there.' Some mumbling. 'In our colours business something is also changing. It is our job to keep the barriers high and we can do that through brand strength, being cheaper, innovations, or a combination of those. If we succeed at that, I'm sure these businesses can provide great value.' A strategy was slowly taking shape.

| SUMMARY |

We have spent a lot of time and effort looking at position in the market, evaluating competitive position, competencies, and industry attractiveness. In a nutshell, to devise your strategy you need to know three things about your segments:

1. Your RMS, which tells you how strong you are in a segment relative to other suppliers.

2. Your competencies, and how well these help you in your segments. Some segments are better served by your competencies than others.

3. The industry attractiveness of a segment or group of segments.

Taken together, these three inputs are your most important clues as to which segments to prioritize and which to de-emphasize.

Now it's time to start looking progressively outward, at the customers and competitors, to obtain final pointers for the strategy before we begin to wrap up and define who we are and where we want to go.

7

WHAT DO THE CUSTOMERS THINK?

Customers are obviously at the heart of your business and the fact that they keep coming back for more means you are doing a few things right. Now is the time to find out what that is, and, occasionally, also what you are less good at. We do so by asking them.

While we were at lunch, I told Jack that afterwards I would show him the result of my customer interviews. Underlining his growing uneasiness about his business, he volunteered to guess what the results would be.

'They'll all say that we are lousy on price and pretty good on everything else. So the only way we could improve our market share is to buy it, to cut into our profits. As you know, lower prices would mean lower profits, a lower share price and an enforced vacation for Jack Mayhew. But I suppose we might as well see the interview results.'

If I had chosen to show Jack the average results of all the interviews, he would not have been too wrong, and he would have remained dismissive. But I knew better than that. I showed him the results by segment, using a simple but effective technique called 'comb analysis'.

First I showed him the results from the US branded mainstream tea business. You will recall that this was a large, important and profitable segment for UTC, but one in which it had been losing market share. Would the customer interviews explain this?

Comb analysis asks the customers first of all to score what is important to them in deciding which supplier to use – their purchase criteria – on a scale of one (unimportant) to five (essential). The results can then display on a chart like that in Illustration 2.44, which shows what was important to the supermarket buyers of branded tea.

It can be seen that price is the most important criterion, scoring a very high 4.9; followed by brand, also very important (4.7); service (responsiveness to the customer and things like delivery efficiency) which was also important (4.0); with packaging (3.8) also quite important; and product innovation (3.5) moderately important. Not surprisingly, the ability to supply proprietary product was almost completely unimportant (1.1) in the branded segment.

'Nothing new there,' commented Jack. I told him that the next stage in comb analysis was to ask the customers to score the client, in this case Universal Tea, on each of the purchase criteria, again on a one (terrible) to five (excellent) scale, and to overlay these scores on the previous chart, as in

ILLUSTRATION 2.44

Segment purchase criteria for branded tea in the US

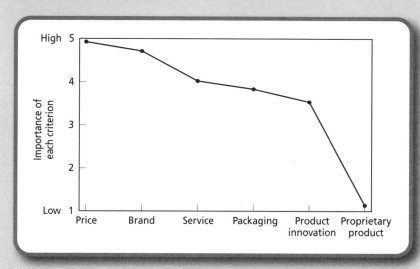

ILLUSTRATION 2.45

Rating of UTC's performance relative to purchase criteria for US branded tea

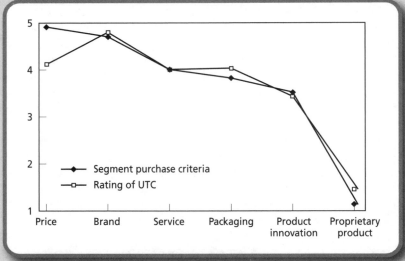

Illustration 2.45. 'Still no surprises,' Jack said. I had to agree: UTC was very close to meeting all the performance criteria of the segment, with the single exception of price.

The third and final stage of comb analysis is to ask the customers to score the client's competitors on a similar one to five scale on each of the criteria, and to further overlay these results, as in Illustration 2.46. 'We can see from this,' I told Jack, 'that the only real selling point for the competition in this segment is price. Unfortunately that is also the most important criterion. UTC appears to have significant advantages in terms of brand and service, which are also important.'

'Now remember,' I went on, 'that this segment is large and important, but UTC has been losing market share. But I conclude from these data that we should be able to do something about that. The gap between our rating and that of the competitor on price is not enormous, and we are at least as good on everything else. My guess is that if we showed a bit more flexibility on price we could get a lot more of the business. We should also stress the fact that our brand and our service are superior to the competition's, so perhaps we do not absolutely have to match their price to win more business.'

'But that would mean lower profits,' objected Jack, 'and what if they cut price still further? Only the customer would win.'

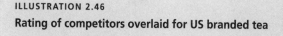

ILLUSTRATION 2.46

Rating of competitors overlaid for US branded tea

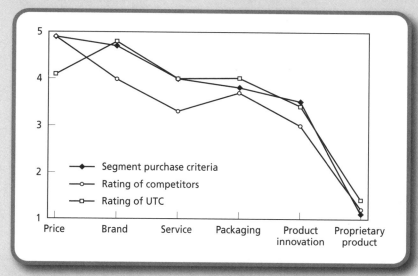

'Profits would not necessarily be lower,' I retorted. 'I think that if we did the sums, given the costs in the business that would not increase with more volume, costs like advertising and all the corporate overheads, not to mention the factory fixed costs, so that we could afford to cut price if we could be fairly sure it would give us more market share. Even if our return on sales dropped a bit, we'd make a much higher return on capital, and a lot more absolute profit, which is what concerns the shareholders.'

'But as you say,' I went on, 'the key is the reaction of the competition. We shouldn't make any final decision until we look at their position and likely behaviour. But bear in mind that our leading competitor, United Foods, has only $150m of sales here compared with our $200m. There is no reason, therefore, why they should have lower costs than us, if we were equally efficient.'

'So, Jack, there are really only two options. Either they are more efficient than us, or they are not. If they are, we can compensate for lower prices by becoming as efficient as them at lowering costs. If they are not more efficient, they must be accepting considerably lower profit margins than we are, and a further reduction in price to stop us getting more business could cut their profit margins to an unacceptable level, or even push them into making losses. We need to understand what United Foods characteristically does when faced with these sorts of decisions, so we can predict what it might do. But either way, we can probably get more volume and also increase our profits simultaneously.'

Without stopping to debate this further, I moved on to report on the second important segment, US private label. Here I saved time by displaying straight away all three sets of results: the segment purchase criteria, the rating of Jack's UTC, and the rating of his main competitor, Cheapco. In this case, the results had Jack jumping out of his chair, demanding to know if I had drawn the lines wrong on Illustration 2.47!

'That can't be right,' exclaimed Jack. 'The chart says that the buyers of private label for the supermarkets value product innovation and proprietary products most of all, even more than price. Our people tell me that the only thing these buyers, especially Big Boy Supermarkets, want is a cheap price. And you've seen for yourself how much money we lose in supplying them, because of the ridiculously low price they demand.'

'I agree that the data are surprising,' I countered, 'but I've double-checked the results of the interviews, and I think there are a number of things here that are interesting and potentially helpful.'

'First, just concentrate on the segment purchase criteria compared with their rating of us. It's interesting that they give us a fairly high rating on price, suggesting that they are surprised at how flexible we are on price. Look partic-

ILLUSTRATION 2.47
Comb analysis of US private label tea

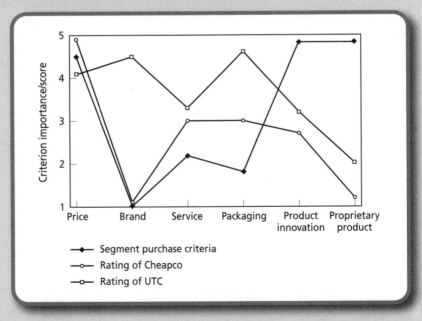

ularly, though, at the rating for our packaging, which at 4.6 is far higher than their purchase criteria at 1.8. This suggests that we might give them cheaper packaging and save ourselves money, without in any way causing them concern. Now look at the surprising importance that they attach to product innovation and proprietary products. What the Big Boy buyer was saying was that they wanted to be able to offer a distinctive product under their own private label, where they would be selling a high quality product at a reasonably high price. This is a change in strategy for them, and they admitted that it is a recent development, but they're very keen on it.'

'Now the interesting thing is, if we look at the rating of Cheapco, the Big Boy buyer is really saying that he couldn't see Cheapco coming up with a proprietary product for them, and although UTC hasn't been at all responsive so far, he sees you as the logical supplier of this.'

By now I had Jack's interest, though not his agreement. 'So,' he queried sarcastically 'you want me to do more unprofitable business with Big Boy, do you?'

'No, but I think it is possible that if you did supply Big Boy with a proprietary product, perhaps a different shape of bag, or product for different regions depending on the water quality, that you could negotiate a profitable contract with much higher prices than on the commodity business. It's also just possible that you could do this in exchange for negotiating slightly higher prices, maybe 5 per cent higher, on the commodity business. They want this proprietary product and you are virtually the only possible supplier. Also, given that Big Boy is very happy with the prices from you and Cheapco, it's likely that their margins on tea are above average and that prices could be edged up a bit. That depends upon the line that Cheapco take, so we can't be confident yet, but it's possible.'

Jack grunted, but I could see the cogs in his brain going round. I decided to move on to the results for the US herb and fruit tea segments, which were so similar that I put them together (Illustration 2.48).

'Now, this is a different picture, but also a very interesting one,' I lectured. 'We see that with the notable exception of price, UTC is meeting the segment's purchase criteria very well. In contrast, our main competitor is rated a five on price, but underperforms the segment's purchase criteria on almost all other dimensions, especially brand strength and product innovation, both of which are very important to the buyers. Note that this segment values product innovation just the same as the private label segment did, but in contrast to the latter, the buyers of fruit and herb teas don't really want proprietary product — they want to sell it under the name of the known brand, which is us.'

'Remember,' I went on, 'the data we showed earlier about these segments. They are extremely profitable for us, fast growing and we are clear leaders, nearly three times bigger than Herbal Health in herb tea and Fruit-Tea Fun in

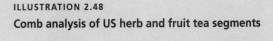

ILLUSTRATION 2.48

Comb analysis of US herb and fruit tea segments

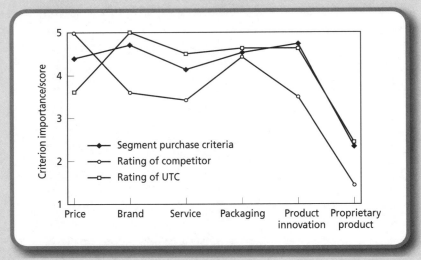

fruit teas. Out of our $21m profits, we make half in these two segments. But we are losing market share in them. And why do you think that is, Jack?'

'Well,' he replied, 'it must be down to price, since we're far better than the competitors on everything else.'

'Right', I said. 'If UTC matched the competitors on price, there would be no reason for anyone to buy from them. Of course, they might undercut us again, and we could get dragged into a price war, so we'd need to understand their likely reactions. But the fact is that we could afford to cut price a bit. Another consideration is that we probably have some bargaining power with our buyers, since they need us for our brand strength and product innovation in particular. It's entirely plausible that we could negotiate higher quantities and regain market share, if we were to shave our price just a bit. The other thing we could do is to speed up the pace of product innovation, and make more of the market in new products, where our competitors would find it harder to respond.'

I decided to draw the session to a close and stared hard at him. 'I think you'll agree, Jack, that we've learned a lot from talking to the customers. But before drawing any definite conclusions, let's take a closer look at the competitors and their freedom to react. I'll see you back here in a week.'

We've seen how customer interviews and comb analysis helped to tailor UTC's offering to the different business segments. You should be able to do the same for your business, and evaluate how customer requirements and your performance vary by segment.

You can take the information from the customer surveys one step further by defining your VALUE DISCIPLINE.

The concept of value discipline can be traced back to management academic Michael Porter's view that firms have three general ways to compete and be successful:

1. *Cost leadership.* Achieving low cost products and services through efficiencies of scale, strict cost control and continuous cost reduction.

2. *Differentiation.* Creating products or services that are unique, allowing higher pricing and profits.

3. *Focus.* Focusing on one customer target and serving this target particularly well, outperforming the *differentiators* and *cost leaders* who aim at the broader market.

In their book *The Discipline of Market Leaders,* Treacy and Wiersema arrived at a similar conclusion. Doing research on customer preferences, they found that customers have three broad kinds of value requirements – best total cost, best product, and best solution. The most successful companies are those that try to deliver such value through matching 'value disciplines', which are similar to Porter's three categories but add a useful twist on them:

Operational excellence means delivering 'best total cost' – a great deal, the lowest overall cost and no surprises. Certainly best total cost could mean the lowest price, but companies that provide durable quality and low maintenance at a modest price, and/or little hassle purchasing the product or service are also examples of best total cost for the customer (total cost is the cost of the product plus the cost the customers add to use it). The famous example is Wal-Mart; others include Toyota (efficient manufacturing, high quality, low maintenance and repair costs) and easyJet and Southwest Airlines (low fares, you-get-what-you-pay-for).

Product leadership delivering 'best product', the latest and greatest product or brand, the hottest technology or innovation. Best-product customers are less concerned with price. Examples include Apple, Intel and Bang & Olufsen in consumer electronics and Louis Vuitton and Gucci in design and fashion.

Customer intimacy delivering 'best solution', or exactly what is needed. Looking for tailored solutions, personalized products and services, and responsiveness to specific needs, 'best solution' customers are not wholly satisfied with standard products or top-of-the-line products as these do not meet their specific requirements. A typical example would be the outsourcing of services, where IBM was long the flag-bearer.

To be successful in a value discipline a company must be committed to delivering just that. You cannot simultaneously optimize your supply chain and streamline manufacturing – to offer low prices and great quality – *and* run a highly innovative R&D and sales organization – to develop the best and latest products – *and* be flexible in production and sales – to deliver customized products or services. You are well advised to stick to one of these three ideas and be outstanding in this one sphere. Of course, you can try to cover more than one base, and many businesses do. But in Porter's useful phrase such companies get 'stuck in the middle' – the result is usually dismal. Each of your departments will be overworked due to numerous and conflicting requests. You will turn out mediocre results in every area and be expensive to boot.

Why do companies continue to try to be everything to everyone? Because they feel more comfortable trying to meet all of their customers' requests rather than to disappoint them by saying 'no' in some cases. The customer is always right, huh?

Wrong thinking. The customer doesn't really want to be right; (s)he wants to be well served. Companies such as Wal-Mart and Apple prove that customers prefer to be delighted in one area, instead of barely satisfied across the board. Customers understand they can't have it all. They do not expect both the lowest price and personalized service, nor do they expect the latest features to come at a bargain. Nobody has ever walked out of the Apple store being upset that great technology and design do not come at Dell prices.

To be successful you need to focus on one value discipline. But while you should become the best in one of the three disciplines, you can not afford to fall too far behind in others. One can charge a premium for novel technology, but not excessively so or people will stick with the older stuff. Equally, while Wal-Mart and Tesco may be offering the lowest prices in the business, they cannot drop their level of service too much below that of service-oriented competitors like WholeFoods. So the trick is to excel and constantly improve in one value discipline, while keeping up-to-standards in the others.

Irrespective of industry, companies dedicated to one particular value discipline are remarkably similar. So, companies dedicated to product leadership in electronics look and operate a lot like product leaders active in chemicals, or mattresses. They have similar cultures, organizations and management styles. The same is true for companies in the other value disciplines.

This means that behind each value discipline, behind the value provided to the customer, there is a specific way of running and organizing your business

(Illustration 2.49). This is the business' operating model – your business processes, your IT and management systems, your company culture. Depending on which value proposition you choose, you should implement the operating model that goes with it (Illustration 2.50).

ILLUSTRATION 2.49

The operating model determines the value delivered to the customers

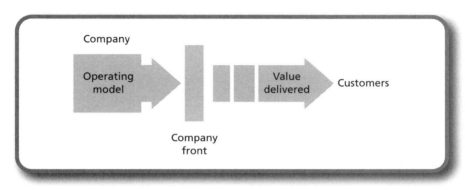

ILLUSTRATION 2.50

Typical attributes of operating models delivering specific values

Discipline	Operational excellence	Product leadership	Customer intimacy
Value	Best total cost	Best product	Best solution
Theme	Low cost relative to competitors	Unique product or brand	Serving a target particularly well
Objectives	High market share, favorable (raw material) costs	Exclusive products and brands	Customized products or services, share of customer's wallet
Mindset	One size fits all	Out-of-the-box	Have it your way
Organization	Hierarchical, centralized	Ad-hoc and organic	Entrepreneurial client teams
Focus on	Supply chain and cost reduction	Innovation and market introduction	Client acquisition and development

Unfortunately, of the three disciplines, executives typically are not keen on operational excellence. Many think it is only about cutting costs. Nothing is further from the truth. Each discipline is as innovative and exciting as the other, and each offers the opportunity to gain market share and make profit in excess of competition. Well carried out, operational excellence is not about penny-pinching but about excellence in managing the supply chain and in using information technology.

To develop a successful strategy, then, you must choose your own value discipline. How? Answer three questions:

1. What are you good at?

2. What do your customers prefer?

3. How large and profitable is the market for each value discipline?

First the easy part: what you are good at? We already determined this in Chapter 5. If your competencies contain terms such as 'low-cost' or 'integrated', you are probably predisposed towards operational excellence. If your strength tends more towards the area of product leadership, your competencies will involve words like 'innovation', 'brand' and 'speed-to-market'. Finally, a customer-intimate predisposition has competencies like 'tailored service' and 'broad product portfolio'.

Focus where you are already strong. For example, UTC – with clear skills in product innovation and branding – should pursue product leadership. The idea of developing a proprietary product for Big Boy's private label sits very well with this.

But your skills and capabilities provide only part of the answer. Think now about what the customers want, and how many of them are looking for each of best total cost, best product or best solution.

Use a survey to find out what your customers want. Define the attributes they look for in their suppliers, and match these with the value disciplines. You have seen how that worked for UTC. Customers said that most important for them was brand and product innovation, then price. The first two can be linked to product leadership, the third to operational excellence.

In the car industry the important attributes today are reliability, repair and maintenance costs and price. All three of these can be easily linked to operational excellence. This is the basis of Toyota's success.

Because industries differ and times change, there is no standard recipe to cling to. Companies have to determine what attributes the customer looks for, and then develop an appropriate offering along one of the three value disciplines.

Keep in mind that in any market there is always room for more than one value discipline, to be provided by different competitors. There will be different customers looking for different value, which cannot be fulfilled by the same suppliers. Thus, while UTC can be the product leader in the tea business, the high importance of price shows there is also room for a competitor supplying a basic product at an unbeatable price.

The only difference is the relative size of those markets. This is the third question to answer. You can see this at work in air travel. There is a market for product leaders such as Singapore Airlines. The market for operational excellence – low fares – is still growing, and is being served by companies such as easyJet and Southwest Airlines. Yet there is also an attractive customer intimate niche, offering to rent your own aircraft, or share the ownership of small jets. Each of these markets is interesting in its own right.

Again, if you are predisposed through strong skills and a customer base that prefers what you stand for, don't try to change to another value discipline. Rather strengthen your existing skills and serve your customers even better. But if you are stuck-in-the-middle, you have no clear skills bias and your customer portfolio is relatively undifferentiated, then find out which area has the most value. Focus there.

How did Addit use the information about its customers?

Using customer data at Addit

Sue and I sat down to discuss what a customer survey could do for Addit. While we discussed the various aspects, Sue said 'You know, I'd find it interesting to know any different requirements between segments, especially if they are substantial. But I don't think that's essential for us. The main problem is that we just try to do it all.'

Indeed, Addit's employees were jumping through hoops for the customers, particularly in the US. On the one hand, the sales and marketing organization was trying to win and keep as many customers as possible, offering customized products and blends. The customers were very happy to engage in this, but generally would not pay for the higher costs. Thus, sales would go up, but not profits.

The proliferation of products was putting strain on manufacturing. The plants tried to work efficiently, but repeatedly had to adjust to specific and last-minute demands. At the same time the R&D group was working on new products and tweaks of existing products for diverse areas. Also it was trying to develop better and cheaper manufacturing processes.

I nodded. 'I agree completely. Addit is just stuck-in-the-middle and it's driving people nuts — and they don't even realize it. If you could just make them focus on doing one thing particularly well, then Addit would make more profit, and everyone would have a more rewarding job for it.'

Sue concurred, 'And probably we can still tailor by segment. But we will get the most mileage out of just knowing what essential needs we must meet.'

In our next strategy group meeting we asked about the key attributes in Addit's industry. Predictably, the first thing brought up by marketing was price, but soon we added delivery reliability and consistency of product quality. It didn't take too long to get the attributes shown in Illustration 2.51, each with one or two value disciplines linked to it.

Next, a market research firm was hired to survey Addit's worldwide customer base. We drew up questions around each attribute, and provided the firm with contact information for customers. To be efficient, we gave them only the 20 per cent of customers who generated roughly 80 per cent of Addit's revenues and profits. Also we added some customers that we had lost to competition, so we would get a picture of the broader market, not just our own customers.

After about two months the results came back and Sue organized a meeting with the strategy group.

First we looked at the importance that customers assigned to each of the attributes (Illustration 2.52).

ILLUSTRATION 2.51

Attributes of Addit's market and associated value discipline

Attribute	Associated value discipline		
	Operational excellence	Product leadership	Customer intimacy
Consistent product quality	X		
Delivery time & reliability	X		X
Product price	X		
Technical support			X
Order placement process	X		
Sales force support		X	X
Broad or customized product range			X
Product innovation		X	

ILLUSTRATION 2.52

Business purchase criteria for Addit's business

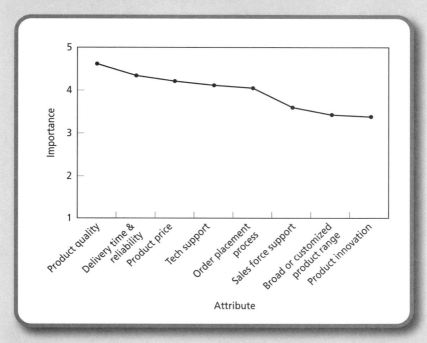

The chart gave a strong clue to what Addit's customers valued most. Out of the five most important attributes, four relate to operational excellence. Price turned out to be third in importance, with (consistent) product quality and delivery time and reliability quoted by customers as their most important concerns.

The attributes typical for the other two value disciplines received lower importance scores. Thus, broad or customized product range, typical for a customer-intimate one-stop-shop, and product innovation – for product leadership – were considered less important. Although the scores of about 3.5 indicated that customers did not find these attributes *unimportant*, clearly they were happy buying different products from different suppliers. Nor did they express a great need for new products.

I told the group: 'What this clearly shows is that your customers are looking for best total cost. They want no surprises with product quality, no hassle with deliveries, easy ordering and a great price. That means Addit should choose operational excellence as the leading motif.'

As you can imagine, this went down very well with the manufacturing managers. They saw an opportunity to end the complexity brought on them by their marketing colleagues. The marketing people were less amused. The sales force support attribute received a third-lowest rank in importance and marketing feared they might be relegated to the role of order-takers. Susan and I had to battle their misgivings.

An interesting discussion revolved around technical support. Customers clearly considered this important, even though it is a customer-intimate-type attribute. Supposing that Addit would choose operational excellence, how would it also provide more technical service? Some managers indicated this would be impossible, since service is so expensive. Others said that it might be feasible if Addit could be low-cost in everything *but* technical service. Still others thought Addit should provide technical support in a low-cost way. Maybe we could give preferred customers access to a frequently-asked-questions database? How about doing the most laborious work in South Africa, India or China? While these were all fine ideas, I asked the managers to hold off for a moment to look at the next comb chart, which showed how well Addit met customer expectations (Illustration 2.53).

ILLUSTRATION 2.53

Rating of Addit's performance relative to purchase criteria

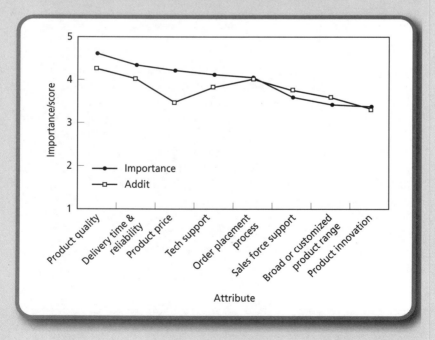

The results were not great. While Addit met customer expectations on the four least important attributes, it was underperforming the four most important ones. The gap was particularly substantial for price, but Addit's underperformance on the two most important parameters was perhaps more disconcerting.

Some relief came from the overlay of Addit's traditional competitors, AdCorp, BonGout and Raben (Illustration 2.54). They were not doing much better. AdCorp and BonGout were almost spitting images of Addit and only Raben was a bit different. It performed better on price – as Addit knew in personal care where Raben and CheapSkills were more flexible on price – but was weaker on technical support.

The really different player revealed itself on next display: CheapSkills. It at once explained the customer's high expectations on price (Illustration 2.55).

CheapSkills – a company still relatively new in the market – underperformed on the lesser attributes of range and innovation, but was selling at a price that spot-on matched customer expectations. In fact, CheapSkills, like so many low-cost suppliers, was setting new standards on price.

ILLUSTRATION 2.54

Rating of Addit's traditional competitors

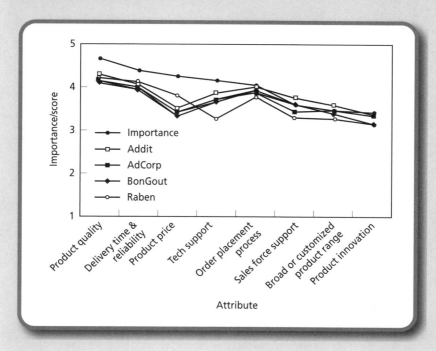

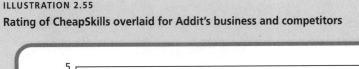

ILLUSTRATION 2.55

Rating of CheapSkills overlaid for Addit's business and competitors

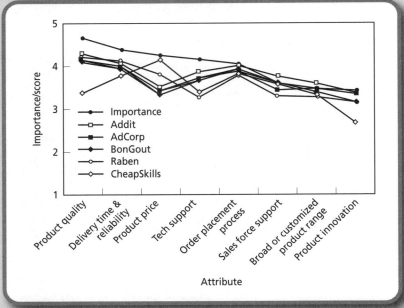

Meanwhile, CheapSkills was not doing any worse than its competitors on delivery, order placement and (surprisingly) technical support. It only underperformed in product quality, explaining why CheapSkills was so far active in the less sophisticated segments (anti-oxidants and personal care).

CheapSkills was raising the bar in operational excellence. The other players would have to shape up.

The mood in the room was mixed. The customer survey had shown that customers were asking for a best total cost type of supplier. To be that kind of supplier, Addit had to change. Worse still, a new and previously underestimated player was making inroads in the market with a sharp proposition: basic products at a great price.

Being the market leader, and with none of its other competitors doing much better, Addit could buy time to improve. But it would take a sustained and focused effort. As you can glean from Addit's competencies and skills (Chapter 5), there is not much that supports an operational excellence approach, or, in fact, any other value discipline. Addit was quite literally all things to all people. The best news was that it was free to choose a new direction.

Before calling it a day, Sue and I wrote down the following conclusions and questions:

Attaining operational excellence:

1. Improve deliveries and quality consistency.
2. Reduce costs to reduce price (can we get away with lower/cheaper product quality?).
3. Find a way to provide technical support cheaply (internet? India?).
4. Trim sales support and product range.

Improving deliveries and product quality would mean two things. First, improving how people worked in customer service and logistics, making order placement simpler and faster. Second, manufacturing would have to focus on producing the most important products in a consistent way. This meant cutting back elsewhere, particularly on Addit's broad product range, which customers did not value anyway.

The second point, on lower or cheaper product quality rested on a hunch. The survey data did not indicate that customers wanted lower quality products. But Sue had a feeling that part of CheapSkills' lower cost was due to lower quality product. If true, this would point to a drastic – but not uncommon – shift in customer requirements: accepting a lesser product, because it comes at a substantially lower price. We would address this point in the next step, about competitors.

Of course, the points about cost reduction, cheap technical support and trimming sales did not meet with cheers. But the customer survey results were corroborating other indications of the same point. Costs and prices had to come down. And as Sue explained, the emergence of CheapSkills in anti-oxidants and personal care showed that it was possible to provide standard products at much lower prices. Addit would have to match that capability to stay on top.

SUMMARY

What do your customers think of you? What value discipline should your business choose? Determine the key attributes and survey the market to work out how to position yourself.

Base your decision on the preferences of your most profitable customers. Serving them better than you have before and better than any competitor could do is your best way forward. But don't forget to check the size and profitability of the market for the other value disciplines. If there is more value in serving those customers, and your skills support that, think hard about whether to make that option the cornerstone of your strategy.

8

WHAT ABOUT THE COMPETITORS?

Modern management thought presents two opposite views on how important it is to analyse competitors. One view is that understanding competitors and how to beat them is at the heart of competitive advantage and strategy. The other is that the important thing is to get on with your own life, learn how to serve customers best and reduce costs, and not worry too much about what anyone else is doing.

Our view is poised nicely between the two extremes. We would never start doing business unit strategy by looking at the competitors, except to help define the segments. The key things to understand from the outset are what your own firm is good at, where it makes the most money, and what your customers think of you. We also agree that it is more important to serve customers and make high returns than it is to 'beat' competitors, and that co-existence and implicit co-operation between competitors (especially if this involves tacit admission of each other's turf and avoidance of head-to-head competition by focusing on separate segments) is often a better route to sustainably high returns than a determination to outdo the opposition.

Our final concession to the 'worry about customers, not competitors' school of thought is to agree that strategy consultants often want to study competitors because they think this is a good thing to do rather than because they have precise and particular questions to answer. Such 'fishing expeditions' are usually a huge waste of time and money.

But in our experience, there is scarcely a business that could not benefit greatly from asking a few specific questions about its competitors. A good source for such questions is the customer survey, particularly those attributes where you find yourself under- or over-performing your competitors.

UTC and Addit were no exceptions. For each of UTC's three main business segments there were one or two questions about competitors that needed answering before we could work out a strategy to boost profits. For Addit, we needed to know a few things concerning competitor costs and their value discipline.

The questions Richard wanted to answer concerning UTC's competitors are shown below. Note that these questions are very focused. Most of the answers, as it happened, came from a relatively straightforward look at relevant data on the web, at the financial documents filed by the competitors, combined with a press search and a few phone interviews with industry observers, brokers and some people within the competitor companies. Richard's report back to Jack a week later is summarized below.

A few things that Jack really needed to know about his competitors

A. US branded tea segment

A1. Is United Foods much more efficient and lower cost in branded tea than Jack's UTC? If so, why and how?

A2. How would United Foods react if UTC lowered its prices and started to regain market share in branded tea?

B. US private label tea segment

B1. Is Cheapco much more efficient and lower cost in private label tea than UTC? If so, why and how?

B2. What would be Cheapco's reaction if UTC raised its prices and attempted to move the general level of prices up?

C. US herbal and fruit tea segments

C1. What is the profitability and relative cost position of Herbal Health and Fruit-Tea Fun, each compared with UTC?

C2. What would be the reaction of each of Herbal Health and Fruit-Tea Fun if UTC moved closer to them on price?

What Richard told Jack about his competitors

A. US branded tea segment

A1. United Foods is making a return on sales of just over 7 per cent in the US branded tea business. Its prices in the supermarkets are on average some 5 per cent below those of UTC. The supermarkets are thought to be earning about 2 per cent higher margin on United Foods tea than on UTC tea. Therefore it seems reasonable to conclude that if United Foods had the same prices as UTC in tea, United Foods' return on sales would be 14 per cent (7 per cent + 5 per cent + 2 per cent). UTC makes roughly 9 per cent return on sales in branded tea, so United Foods has costs about 5 per cent below those of UTC.

Note, however, that United Foods has branded tea sales of only $150m in the US, compared with $200m for UTC. Normally, this would give

UTC a cost advantage because of economies of scale, especially in marketing, that would be worth about 2 per cent return on sales.

It follows that the potential for UTC to reduce costs is in excess of 5 per cent of sales, with a rough target of 7 per cent.

UTC is losing market share to United Foods. Judging by the customer analysis, this is solely due to price – the lower prices being offered by United Foods to both consumers and to the supermarkets. Because UTC's brand, 5 Unicorns, is superior to that of United Foods, and because UTC's service to the supermarkets is better, it follows that market share loss could be arrested without completely matching United Foods' price.

If United Foods did not react to UTC lowering prices, it seems reasonable to conclude that a 4 per cent price cut (split between the consumer and the supermarkets) would stabilize market shares, that is, stop the loss of market share from UTC to United Foods. A 7 per cent price cut should lead to UTC regaining market share from United Foods, again in the absence of the latter also cutting price.

A2. United Foods is a well-run company, but it has publicly declared that it will seek to increase its earnings per share and stockholder dividends by a minimum of 10 per cent a year. Analysts expect that to be difficult for United Foods to achieve this year because of problems in the banana market. Tea is expected to account a quarter of United Foods' profits this year. It appears vital for United Foods to maintain its tea profits this year, and price-cutting would make a severe dent in these.

It seems reasonable to think, therefore, that unless UTC began to take a large volume of sales away from United Foods, the latter would be unlikely to cut prices.

B. **US private label tea segment**

B1. By the same process of analysis as in Al it seems that Cheapco is a staggering 10 per cent lower cost than UTC in private label tea. A lot of this difference, perhaps up to 3 per cent, is due to the cheaper packaging used by Cheapco. As seen in the comb analysis, buyers place no value on UTC's more expensive packaging. UTC could therefore raise its margins, or cut its prices, by about 3 per cent almost overnight by a change in its packaging purchasing policy.

There is no discernible difference in prices between Cheapco and UTC in this segment.

There is an opportunity for UTC to lower its costs by up to 10 per cent. This could turn a business losing 5 per cent on sales into one making 5 per cent on sales, within say two years.

Cheapco currently makes 6 per cent return on sales on private label tea.

B2. From sources I cannot reveal, I am fairly confident that a 2 per cent price rise by UTC would be followed by Cheapco.

C. US herbal and fruit tea segments

C1. Herbal Health has a return on sales of 9 per cent (UTC: 14 per cent in herb tea), and Fruit-Tea Fun a return on sales of 8 per cent (UTC: 12 per cent in fruit tea). Both companies price about 5 per cent below UTC.

It is likely, therefore, that each competitor's costs are roughly the same as those of UTC.

UTC has a scale advantage, being nearly three times larger than either Herbal Health or Fruit-Tea Fun. This advantage should be worth about 4 per cent return on sales.

There may well, therefore, be the opportunity to reduce UTC costs by up to 4 per cent.

C2. Moving closer to the competitors in price would probably reverse the loss of market share, unless they followed down in price. Neither company can afford to do that. Herbal Health has just floated on the stock market and Fruit-Tea Fun plans to do the same. For the next two years, both companies need to show steadily increasing profits, and they have no other businesses.

Addit and its competitors

The questions that needed answering for Addit centred around Addit's main segments: animal and human nutrition, human food, and personal care. What were Addit's costs relative to its competitors?

In the first place, Addit's costs are determined by the raw materials it buys. The proportion of such costs can vary widely by industry, but for Addit it amounts to as much as 59 per cent of its total sales revenues (Illustration 2.56). This money is spent on a great variety of basic chemicals that are converted and packaged into final products in Addit's plants.

Operating these plants constitutes Addit's second large cost item, over £52 million, 19 per cent of sales. A lesser part of Addit's cost is attributable to the SAR costs — costs of selling and marketing, of general management overhead, and R&D — totaling 14 per cent of sales.

With this in mind:

1. On average, what percentage of costs do competitors spend on raw materials? On manufacturing? And on SAR?

ILLUSTRATION 2.56
Addit's cost breakdown

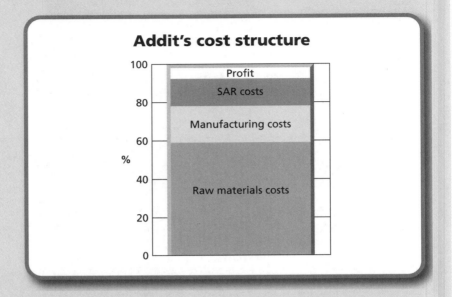

Addit's cost structure

2. In personal care, how can Raben and CheapSkills offer lower prices? Do they compete with a lower quality product?
3. In anti-oxidants, how can CheapSkills offer lower prices?
4. How would Addit and Raben react if Addit cut its prices?
5. Which value discipline do Addit's competitors pursue?

Answers to the cost questions came through a mix of product research (analyzing samples of competitor products), market feedback (anecdotes and answers from customer) and specialized cost models. Research also involved government filings, what Addit knew about competitor sales and readily available data such as average salaries and raw material costs in different regions of the world.

For the value discipline determination, an objective outsider was asked to evaluate the performance of Addit and its competitors. Here are the results.

1. Cost structure

Addit determined the cost breakdown in the additive industry for three cases – the industry average, a best-in-class Western-style supplier, and a low-cost player such as CheapSkills (Illustration 2.57).

The industry on average is more profitable than Addit. This is due to lower costs in manufacturing and SAR. Addit is currently at a serious disadvantage even compared with its traditional competitors.

ILLUSTRATION 2.57

Addit and industry cost structure

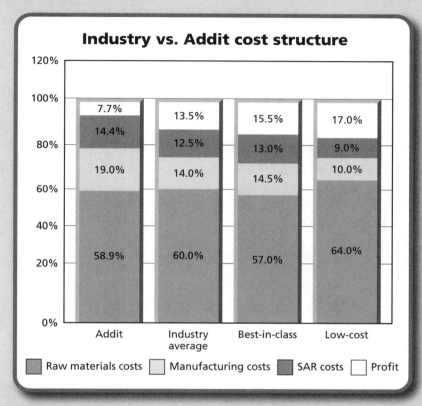

Industry vs. Addit cost structure

	Addit	Industry average	Best-in-class	Low-cost
Profit	7.7%	13.5%	15.5%	17.0%
SAR costs	14.4%	12.5%	13.0%	9.0%
Manufacturing costs	19.0%	14.0%	14.5%	10.0%
Raw materials costs	58.9%	60.0%	57.0%	64.0%

Raw materials costs ■   Manufacturing costs □   SAR costs ■   Profit □

Low-cost suppliers such as CheapSkills are more profitable still, even though they spend a higher percentage of their revenue on raw materials.[3] But this is more than compensated for by lower manufacturing and SAR costs.

Why are Addit's costs higher? This is simply a matter of AVERAGE COSTING and AVERAGE PRICING (see the Glossary). Incumbent suppliers such as Addit have many 'speciality' products for which they do not charge a high enough price. The additional costs are spread over the bulk of standard products, raising Addit's average manufacturing and SAR costs. In contrast, the low-cost

---

[3] Supposing that raw material costs are the same 55 per cent for a low-cost and a standard company, but the price is 100 cents for the standard company, and 90 cents for the low-cost company, then the raw material cost percentage translates to 55/100 = 55% for the standard company and 55/90 = 61% for the low-cost company

suppliers only supply standard products, and they know very well what it costs to make them and how to price them profitably.

2. Personal care

Customer information and product testing confirmed that CheapSkills was supplying a lower quality product. Customers accept this because of the price discount. Raben is matching the prices of CheapSkills to prevent loss of market share. Raben was rumoured to be field-testing a low-quality product.

3. Anti-oxidants

As mentioned earlier, CheapSkills is able to offer low prices through lower cost in manufacturing and overhead.

4. How would competitors react if Addit cut prices in personal care?

4a. CheapSkills appears to be an opportunistic player. The company has limited production assets and wants to generate the most revenue with it. CheapSkills has substantial sales outside of the additives market and is not – or not yet – very dependent on the additives market. If Addit lowered its prices, CheapSkills would make less profit and would be less vigorous in the pursuit of personal care customers. Most likely it would then manufacture other, more profitable products with outlets outside Addit's markets. The situation in anti-oxidants should be similar.

4b. Raben is different. It's been in the market for years, and it respects the presence and market share of traditional competitors such as Addit. Raben is well aware that its main competitors have heavy investments and that nobody should be forced to lose too much market share or take desperate measures that will hurt everyone.

Raben has no history of aggressive moves. It is likely that Raben has been picking up customers from Addit due to its lower pricing, which in turn was its reaction to losing ground to CheapSkills. If Addit reduced prices to a level that would bar CheapSkills from further expansion, this would probably not be followed by renewed price cuts from Raben, as long as Addit didn't poach Raben's customers.

5. Value disciplines

Addit was thinking of choosing operational excellence as its core discipline, but also wanted to assess which competitors might do the same.

All players were evaluated on their current skills and strengths, including such things as 'strength of technology', 'management commitment', 'manufacturing capability' and 'innovativeness'. The data was aggregated as Illustration 2.58. The size of a bubble indicates the company's total sales. The position of a bubble in the triangle tells how well each company meets the three broad value requirements – the closer to a corner, the better a company meets that requirement.

ILLUSTRATION 2.58

Value discipline of Addit and its competitors in the food and feed additives industry

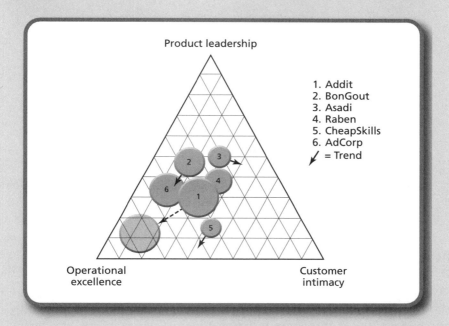

Illustration 2.58 shows how Addit and most of its competitors are stuck in the middle, competing in the same, undifferentiated space with no strong leaning towards any of the three value disciplines. This confirms the customer survey. Asadi, a small player, is perhaps closest to best product, based on a small but interesting market for speciality additive products and solutions. Cheap-Skills is moving ever closer to operational excellence (with a customer intimacy 'twang' to it), as is BonGout, although from much further away.

Addit's choice for operational excellence was warranted, but would not eliminate competition. While Addit makes a dash for the open field, it should expect similar moves from CheapSkills and maybe BonGout and AdCorp. But the company that best meets the customer's best total cost preferences would reap the rewards. The race was on.

| SUMMARY |

What specific questions do you need to answer about your competitors? Try to understand the attributes in the customer survey where competitors do better or worse than you – and why.

9

SHOULD YOU DO SOMETHING ELSE?

At this point you may be asking yourself: but isn't strategy also about doing other things?

This was certainly what most corporate headquarters busied themselves with in the 1950s and 1960s. At that time, DIVERSIFICATION was the central edict for all companies. Spurred on by the ANSOFF MATRIX (Illustration 2.59), firms were stimulated to take their products into new markets, develop new products for existing markets, or push into new markets with new products altogether. This phase in strategy thinking can be credited with some of the most spectacular failures in business. It is also to blame for raising a generation or two of managers who believe that strategy is all about doing new things, and pretty dismal at making money from it.

ILLUSTRATION 2.59
Ansoff matrix for business development

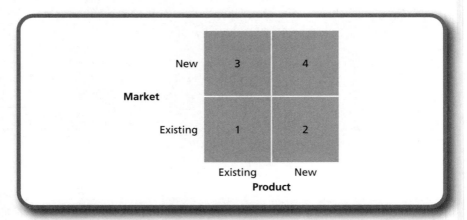

Nowadays the role of 'diversification' has been taken over by its cousin 'innovation'. Inspired by the stunning growth in the internet industry, traditional companies are told to become more 'innovative'. They should develop new technologies or completely new business models, move into new markets and acquire unrelated businesses to boost their own. Today, as then, many such moves are ill-advised even for corporations with financial staying power. Business units are even less likely to succeed.

Let's make ourselves perfectly clear: we are not against innovation. Far from it! But in being innovative, we believe most business units need not go beyond their existing business. If you are in a reasonably attractive industry (see Chapter 6) and your market is expanding, all you need to do is pursue maximum growth. Innovate existing products for your current customers. It's not just infinitely easier, it is also a sure road to success.

But there are powerful forces at work to make you believe otherwise. Expanding into new areas where you have little experience, trying to acquire new customers, implementing an innovative business model, all of this is not easy and probably makes you look for help. Consultants and bankers are more than willing to assist you with market research, product development, or an acquisition. All this is very expensive, it can take years, and only you are bothered by the need to make a return on your money spent. Meanwhile, the base business may wither for lack of attention and investment.

What's in a word?

When I brought up the question of innovation, Sue reacted dismissively. 'We are not going to innovate at all,' she said. 'We have a lot to do already: why would I want to burden myself with yet another thing that we need to manage?' After which she added 'and we should stop that project on additives for plants. That's been going on forever and they're getting nowhere with it.' Sue was referring to a business development project to sell new, special additives to boost plant growth. The project had been plagued by technical difficulties and poor market reception.

Since I have a background in research, I knew what Sue meant. But I also knew what was going on in Addit's R&D department, and what some of the managers were thinking.

'You're right,' I said. 'But look at it this way. Innovation can be a number of things. You can innovate for your existing customers, for example by providing better vitamins, or reducing the costs of the chemical processes by which you make them.' Sue nodded. 'Fine,' she said, 'that's what R&D should work on then.'

'As you know,' I continued, 'there is also 'blue sky research'. Certain firms – such as 3M – are very good at that. It's how IBM developed the PC.' Sue looked at me sideways and shook her head. 'But it takes a lot of money and perseverance, and it's not really recommended for business units.'

'But blue sky research can also mean that you develop something new around your most important products and technology – like a whole new, cheaper way to make vitamin C. I think that's important, it's how the CD was developed. You know Philips, right? They made turntables and at the time were also a distributor of records. So they developed a successor for the record. Very smart and successful.'

I continued: 'Same for you, if you were to develop biotechnology processes to produce vitamins and colours more cheaply than through your current chemical processes.'

I put a copy of the Ansoff matrix (see Illustration 2.59) on Sue's desk, and pointed at the lower left quadrant. 'So you can look for innovation among your existing products and technology here, and also do some blue sky things. In this quadrant (I pointed at the upper right quadrant) are way-out innovations. That's not for Addit.'

'Then there is innovation of your business itself. You could try to enter new business segments with existing or very related products. That's where the plant additive project fits. And the new extracts is an example where you've been successful at that.' I pointed at the top-right Ansoff quadrant. Sue looked as if she was surprised Addit had been successful at a development at all. 'Hey,' I reacted, 'some people even say that geographic expansion is innovation. You did that.' Sue rolled her eyes.

'Finally, you could offer new products for your existing customers. That's over here,' as I pointed at the bottom-right quadrant. 'In a way, you did that when you came up with the sweetener. The customer was already buying vitamins and you developed a sweetener for them.'

'So, Addit is doing a lot of things, many of which could be called "innovation". The point is that the strategy has to provide focus to all of those activities. You have to decide what you will and won't do.'

'For example, many managers support Addit's push into the plant additives field. They think if it was a success, it would be big business. They could be right.'

'So you think it is OK?'

'No. I agree it's too big a stretch, but that's not my main objection.'

Sue glanced at me suspiciously 'So what is?'

'I think you need your energy to fix things in your main areas. You agreed that operational excellence is the best approach for Addit, that's a big thing. It will require effort, time and money. You need to make your processes less complex, more reliable. Most of all, you need to make them cheaper. High-volume products and flawless manufacturing … that should be the central theme for R&D and business development.'

'So you agree with me after all!'

'Well, if you agree that that's innovation, absolutely. Shall I talk to the managers?' Sue just grunted.

The safest and wisest thing is usually not to go beyond what you are good at today. Sure, make your products more innovative, bring out improvements that customers ask for, build market share, but don't 'do' something else.

What are the arguments to go beyond today's business? Three are usually advanced:

1. You are doing brilliantly and feel that your management and employees have time and energy to take up something else.

2. You are doing pretty well across the board and you have a competence that's in demand. It can be used elsewhere to make more money.

3. You are the market leader but your most important business segments are stagnant or contracting due to industry developments.

The first reason is the most compelling argument to branch out. It sounds great and sometimes it is. But it's often a trap. The core business can always be made better, and this is usually more profitable than diversification.

The second rationale is tricky. Competence-based expansion requires a lot of effort and financial staying power. Success is certainly possible, but many businesses have a rose-tinted view of their competencies. And the competencies will typically give a better return in the base business where they were developed.

As for the third reason, if you are the leader in a stagnant or declining industry, there is really nothing wrong with harvesting the value and managing the decline. It's a sure way to generate lots of value. It avoids the sizeable costs of trying to do something that will take quite some time to master, and where competitors are usually better placed. Let your owners, corporate parent or shareholders decide where to reinvest that money.

But let's assume that we haven't put you off. For whatever reason, you're determined to go beyond your current business.

OK, here's a recipe:

◆ *Make a shortlist of interesting activities, as closely related as possible to what you do today.*

◆ *Conduct an industry attractiveness analysis to determine entry barriers, financial returns and the intensity of competition (see Chapter 6).*

◆ *Check how well your competences support each idea.*

◆ *Survey the market to find out what attributes are important. Delete any idea that doesn't fit your value discipline.*

◆ *Narrow the ideas down to one or two activities where you may have the best chance.*

◆ *Consider finding a partner to complement you either in market access or in product/technology know-how.*

Done all that?

Now apply relentless focus. Don't take on another activity until you're sure of success or defeat. You should reach that point within three to five years. If you don't get there in time, stop!

10

WHO ARE WE? WHAT WILL WE DO?

We now have all the essential pieces of the strategy puzzle, and it's that exciting time when we can put them together.

First focus on the question of who you are and what you're good at doing – according to the market. Where do your customers rate you highly and allow you to make great profits? Focus also implies knowing what you are *not* so good at – where competitors are better and you make mediocre or poor returns.

As an illustration, let's recount what some companies who have been through our strategy process have concluded:

'*We are great at supplying high margin, branded stationery items in Europe, delivering high quality product quickly. We cannot be efficient or low enough in cost for lower margin or unbranded product and we are not operationally effective in the US or the Far East.*'

'We are excellent at product invention and innovation. We are poor at market-ing and inefficient at manufacturing.'

'We're good at churning out high volume, standard products at low cost. When we go up-market or try to meet special requirements we fall flat on our face.'

'We can please customers who have rigorous engineering requirements. We get bored and slow when it comes to satisfying standard needs.'

'We are skilled at project management on complex, high value projects. We have no advantage in terms of product, brand or geography. But our people love meeting customers and delivering exactly what they want, fast. We prosper because our particular customers love us.'

What did Addit decide?

Decision time at Addit

Addit was reaching the end of its strategy journey. Sue and the team were ready to make decisions. A week earlier I had provided everyone with a binder of the information that we'd gathered, and all the graphs and tables.

The binder also held a few new charts, including the table shown in Illus-tration 2.60. This table summarizes Addit's current performance by business segment, in an 80/20 manner. It's easy to make. Just order your business seg-ments by decreasing ROS, and then calculate the cumulative sales and profit from each of the segments. (Our software generates this table automatically.)

Almost 90 per cent of Addit's profits are generated by the top eight business segments which comprise only 38 per cent of sales. Illustration 2.61 shows a graph of the data.

The top eight segments describe what is good about Addit today and this analysis was used as the basis for a group discussion. Blending in the conclu-sions from the customer survey and the skills and competencies gave us a summary of Addit's identity and strategic position :

Addit:

◆ Is the market leader in vitamins and colour additives for the food, feed and personal care industry worldwide; it has specific additive know-how, but the most important customers do not need that.

◆ Provides blends globally, and supports blends customers in North America and Europe with essential know-how.

ILLUSTRATION 2.60

80/20 analysis with strategic conclusions of Addit's market segments

Code	Segment	Sales (£m)	Profit (£m)	ROS (%)	% of NS	% of profit	Cumulative Sales (£m)	Profit	% of sales	% of profit
4100	Proprietary blends	10,036	3,039	30.3%	3.6%	14.2%	10,036	3,039	3.6%	14.2%
4200	Custom blends	4,061	887	21.9%	1.5%	4.1%	14,096	3,927	5.1%	18.4%
2110	*Vitamins: Food and beverages*	*14,661*	*3,086*	*21.1%*	*5.3%*	*14.4%*	*28,757*	*7,013*	*10.4%*	*32.8%*
2120	*Vitamins: Supplements*	*23,650*	*4,498*	*19.0%*	*8.5%*	*21.0%*	*52,407*	*11,511*	*18.9%*	*53.8%*
2210	*Colors: Food*	*20,188*	*3,031*	*15.0%*	*7.3%*	*14.2%*	*72,595*	*14,542*	*26.2%*	*68.0%*
2230	*Colors: Pharmaceuticals*	*4,388*	*623*	*14.2%*	*1.6%*	*2.9%*	*76,983*	*15,165*	*27.8%*	*70.9%*
2220	*Colors: Beverages*	*8,434*	*1,112*	*13.2%*	*3.0%*	*5.2%*	*85,418*	*16,277*	*30.9%*	*76.1%*
1200	Feed:Pre-mixers	21,262	2,562	12.0%	7.7%	12.0%	106,679	18,839	38.5%	88.1%
2600	Other: Human nutrition	4,938	479	9.7%	1.8%	2.2%	111,617	19,318	40.3%	90.3%
5300	Other: Non-food citric acid	17,137	1,558	9.1%	6.2%	7.3%	128,754	20,876	46.5%	97.6%
5600	Other: Distributors	16,383	1,391	8.5%	5.9%	6.5%	145,137	22,267	52.4%	104.1%
4300	Standard blends	8,589	505	5.9%	3.1%	2.4%	153,726	22,772	55.5%	106.5%
1100	Feed: Pet food	13,717	625	4.6%	5.0%	2.9%	167,443	23,398	60.5%	109.4%
5100	Other: Intermediates	15,817	606	3.8%	5.7%	2.8%	183,260	24,003	66.2%	112.2%
3000	Personal care	25,588	938	3.7%	9.2%	4.4%	208,847	24,942	75.5%	116.6%
1300	Feed: Integrated manufacturers	13,318	293	2.2%	4.8%	1.4%	222,165	25,234	80.3%	118.0%
5200	Other: Plastic additives	15,618	(310)	−2.0%	5.6%	−1.5%	237,783	24,924	85.9%	116.5%
2400	Sweeteners	23,513	(1,753)	−7.5%	8.5%	−8.2%	261,296	23,171	94.4%	108.3%
5400	Other: Paint additives	5,992	(471)	−7.9%	2.2%	−2.2%	267,288	22,700	96.6%	106.1%
5500	Other: Specialities	3,280	(320)	−9.8%	1.2%	−1.5%	270,568	22,380	97.8%	104.6%
2300	Anti-oxidants	3,628	(410)	−11.3%	1.3%	−1.9%	274,196	21,970	99.1%	102.7%
2500	New extracts	2,593	(580)	−22.4%	0.9%	−2.7%	276,789	21,390	100.0%	100.0%

◆ Supplies a sweetener to an important global customer.

◆ Supplies a mixed bag of other products outside key areas, but cannot hope to become a serious player.

◆ Is a comparatively expensive supplier that is stuck in the middle; its customers look for an operational excellence offering and in some important areas returns are under pressure from cheaper competition.

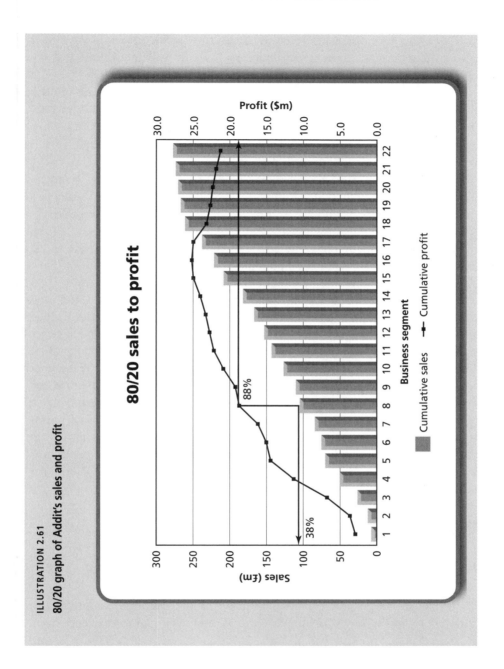

ILLUSTRATION 2.61
80/20 graph of Addit's sales and profit

80/20 sales to profit

Profit ($m)

Sales (£m)

Business segment

Cumulative sales   Cumulative profit

Once you have discovered and articulated the specific source of your company's success, or where it is most successful, there are three things that you *could* do, only two of which are sensible.

First, most people's instinct is to correct their weaknesses: We are good in Europe but not in the US, so, let's sort out the US. This usually ends in tears. There are generally good, deep-rooted reasons for failure in the US (or wherever). It normally requires a lot of time, energy, skill, money and luck to turn bad into good. It's typically not worth the effort and risk.

Second, further enhance your areas of strength. Take what is very good and make it excellent. Take what is better than competitors can do, and make it so much better that they give up entirely. Take something that is excellent by local standards and make it world-beating. Take something that is excellent but brittle, and dependent on a few people, and make it broader-based and so deeply rooted in the company's mentality and way of doing business that it could survive the departure of the current experts and leaders.

Third, focus on the functions, parts of the VALUE CHAIN, products and/or markets that really play to your strengths, gain market share and sales in these areas and migrate to other areas. For example, you may be very good at developing and marketing new products, but not at manufacturing them. Outsource the manufacturing. Or, as in the case of Addit, you are really good at making and selling a few things very well. Focus there. It may be that only 20 per cent of your sales are in the areas of real strength, though these generate 60 per cent of your contribution and 90 per cent of your fully costed profits. In that case, aim to migrate, over time, out of the 80 per cent of sales that do not play to your strengths. Plan so that in five-ten years, your 20 per cent of profitable sales have been tripled, the 80 per cent of unprofitable sales eliminated, and the surplus cost associated with the latter also eliminated. You will have a smaller, simpler, more focused business, and profits nearly three times greater.

Finally, formulate three things:

1. Your MISSION – a short and simple proclamation of what your company does (or is supposed to do).

2. Your VISION – a similar proclamation of the successful company that you aspire to be, the way you will make money and meet customer expectations.

3. Your strategy – four to eight statements that explain how to get from who you are today to what you want to be in the future, and that you can achieve in the coming three to five years.

Keep these simple and succinct. Less is more. Avoid ambiguity. Everybody has to understand exactly what you are going to do, and what not. This is what you will work from in the coming years, what you will use as the yardstick to measure progress.

Share this with your employees – spend time to make sure everyone understands. Doing all this strategy work and coming up with your vision and strategy is quite an achievement. But ultimately you have to rely on the talent in your organization to make it happen. If you don't state your insights in a clear, crisp manner, and get it understood and acted on at every level in your organization, all your work is in vain.

Addit stakes its claim for the future

Having defined what characterized Addit, Sue decided where to focus in the future, starting by categorizing each of Addit's segments, according to profitability, as 'A', 'B' or 'C/D'.

The eight most profitable segments were classified as A priorities. Until now these segments had received only average attention. It was decided to expand these segments aggressively – management, marketing and sales, and R&D would spend much more time on them.

The group was concerned that aggressive growth might lead to a price war. Given their investments, none of the traditional competitors could afford to lose significant sales. Sue calmed the fears: 'By "expand aggressively" we do not mean to go about like mad-men taking share. That *would* provoke a reaction from our competitors. We don't want that at all.'

'But we do want to make sure we grow more than all the others. What's available is the annual volume growth. If the whole market grows 5 per cent, then we can get most or all of that, without anyone else losing volume.'

'Now in some cases we can do still more, and Paul, the segmentation that you came up with is the key to success!' Paul looked surprised.

Sue continued 'Remember that in each of the three feed segments we sell the same products, and that the contribution margin of these segments is comparable.' (See Illustration 2.12.) We also know that the pre-mixers segment is the most profitable of the three, because it requires less service from sales, tech support, and R&D.' (See Illustration 2.16.)

'Now, if we carefully drop our share in the least profitable segments, and substitute it with similar sales in the blends segment, the net effect for our competitors' volume, sales and contribution margin would be hardly noticeable. I'm assuming that they do not look beyond CM, just like we didn't until now.'

The group liked this. It was a cunning plan, though not easy to execute. But Paul and Hank were in for a challenge. 'We can try a few customers and see what happens,' said Paul. On that note we moved on to the next set of segments.

These were the remaining segments where Addit made a profit, though not as high as in the first eight. Comprising about 42 per cent of sales and 30 per cent of profits, management, R&D and sales attention would be reduced, though market share should be retained. These segments were classified as 'B', or 'Maintain', although strategic considerations could still change this verdict.

Even though classified as 'B', the profits of these segments were inadequate, because of Addit's high costs. Cost reductions were essential.

Finally, all the loss-making segments, six in total, were classified as C/D, 'Harvest' or 'Exit'. These segments would have to prove their worth in the strategic review.

ILLUSTRATION 2.62

Initial prioritization of Addit business segments

A: Expand aggressively		B: Maintain		C/D: Harvest/Exit	
Proprietary blends		Other: Human nutrition		Other: Plastic additives	
Custom blends		Other: Non-food citric acid		Sweeteners	
Vitamins: Food & beverages		Other: Distributors		Other: Paint additives	
Vitamins: Supplements		Standard blends		Other: Specialities	
Colors: Food		Feed: Pet food		Anti-oxidants	
Colors: Pharmaceuticals		Other: Intermediates		New extracts	
Colors: Beverages		Personal care			
Feed: Pre-mixers		Feed: Integrated manufacturers			
Total sales	38.5%	Total sales	41.7%	Total sales	19.7%
Total profit	88.1%	Total profit	29.9%	Total profit	−18.0%

The next task was to see whether this profit-based classification backed up the strategic information. Sue and I had prepared another table for the strategy binder, showing for each segment Addit's market position, industry attractiveness and the extent to which it was supported by internal skills and capabilities (Illustration 2.63).

First we looked at the 'A' segments.

Whereas Addit's market position and skill strength was good in each of the eight segments, the industry attractiveness of the colour segments flashed a warning. The industry was not very attractive, chiefly due to lower entry barriers (CheapSkills?) and the comparatively higher bargaining power of

ILLUSTRATION 2.63

Addit strategic conclusions by business segment

Code	Segment	Sales	Profitability	Market position	Industry attractiveness	Skills strength	Priority
4100	Proprietary blends	10,036	Very high	Good	Competitive	Very good	A
4200	Custom blends	4,061	Very high	Good	Competitive	Very good	A
2110	*Vitamins: Food & beverages*	*14,661*	*Very high*	*Good*	*Attractive*	*Good*	A
2120	*Vitamins: Supplements*	*23,650*	*High*	*Good*	*Attractive*	*Good*	A
2210	*Colors: Food*	*20,188*	*Fairly high*	*Good*	*Not very attractive*	*Good*	A
2230	*Colors: Pharmaceuticals*	*4,388*	*Fairly high*	*Good*	*Not very attractive*	*Good*	A
2220	*Colors: Beverages*	*8,434*	*Fairly high*	*Good*	*Not very attractive*	*Good*	A
1200	Feed: Pre-mixers	21,262	Fairly high	OK	Attractive	Good	A
2600	Other: Human nutrition	4,938	OK	–	–	Good	B
5300	Other: Non-food citric acid	17,137	OK	Poor	Not very attractive	Moderate	B
5600	Other: Distributors	16,383	OK	Good	–	Good	B
4300	Standard blends	8,589	Poor	Good	Competitive	Very good	B
1100	Feed: Pet food	13,717	Poor	Good	Attractive	Good	B
5100	Other: Intermediates	15,817	Poor	OK but deteriorating	Unattractive	Moderate	B
3000	Personal care	25,588	Poor	OK but deteriorating	Not very attractive	Good	B
1300	Feed: Integrated manufacturers	13,318	Poor	Good	Attractive	Good	B
5200	Other: Plastic additives	15,618	Loss-making	Poor	Attractive	Weak	?
2400	Sweeteners	23,513	Loss-making	OK but deteriorating	Attractive	Moderate	?
5400	Other: Paint additives	5,992	Loss-making	Weak and deteriorating	Competitive	Weak	?
5500	Other: Specialities	3,280	Loss-making	Poor	–	Weak	?
2300	Anti-oxidants	3,628	Loss-making	Weak	Not very attractive	Moderate	?
2500	New extracts	2,593	Loss-making	Very weak but improving	Attractive	Moderate	?

customers. Should Addit spend a lot of effort in this area? There was a high risk of insufficient return, so the colours segments were reclassified as a 'B' priority: 'Maintain'. Addit would grow with the market and reduce cost, and be able to reduce price and defend its leadership position.

Next up for discussion was the 'competitive' attractiveness rating of two of the blends segments. The proprietary and custom blends were very profitable and, given Addit's good market position and strong skills, deserved to be expanded outright.

Then the eight 'Maintain' segments were evaluated. As a rule, we would maintain and protect our shares, reduce R&D and sales and technical support, and hold back on investments. But was this approach supported by the other information?

It was, except in two of the B segments, which were reprioritized. One was non-food citric acid. The segment had moderate profitability, but a poor position in a market that's not very attractive. That suggested exit. But the segment had a good deal of asset sharing with citric acid made for food and feed usage. The group eventually decided to harvest this segment – halt development efforts, stop new sales effort, reduce costs and gradually raise prices.

The other relatively weak segment was intermediates – Addit had a fair but declining share in an unattractive industry. Like non-food citric acid, this segment was not in the core area of food, feed and personal care. The group decided to harvest this segment too, cutting sales and R&D efforts, and raising some prices.

Finally the C/D segments, starting with sweeteners and new extracts. These were both in Addit's core food and feed markets, and in attractive industries. Addit held a moderately good position in sweeteners, and was growing fast in extracts. It was decided to classify these segments as 'A', to attain scale quickly and improve position. Higher sales would spread the costs in this area over a larger volume and make the segment profitable.

In plastic and paint additives, the managers believed they had no chance. These sales were just a sideline; much larger competitors ruled these markets. It was decided to cut effort to the minimum, and look for an opportunity to sell the segment, or sell finished product to a wholesaler.

Finally, and most controversially, came anti-oxidants. All the strategic indicators flashed warnings – a weak market position in a not very attractive industry, with only modest skills. Yet marketing argued that anti-oxidants were vital in any food and feed product. Sue was dubious: 'We are so small and these sales are so small. That whole segment is small.' Marketing and manufacturing supported each other. Perhaps with effort and focus it would be possible to make this a segment like colours? Eventually Sue gave in: it was agreed to make this a priority segment, as long as manufacturing reduced costs and marketing raised sales. Illustration 2.64 summarizes the decisions.

ILLUSTRATION 2.64

Final prioritization of Addit business segments

A: Expand aggressively	B: Maintain	C: Harvest	D: Exit
Proprietary blends	Colors: Food	Other: Non-food citric acid	Other: Plastic additives
Custom blends	Colors: Pharmaceuticals	Other: Specialities	Other: Paint additives
Vitamins: Food & beverages	Colors: Beverages	Other: Intermediates	
Vitamins: Supplements	Other: Human nutrition		
Feed: blends	Other: Distributors		
Sweeteners	Standard pre-mixers		
New extracts	Feed: Pet food		
Anti-oxidants	Personal care		
	Feed: Integr. manuf.		
Total sales 37.4%	Total sales 42.6%	Total sales 12.2%	Total sales 7.8%
Total profit 53.0%	Total profit 43.5%	Total profit 7.2%	Total profit −3.7%

After the meeting Sue and I reached a strategic synthesis:

Mission: To provide no-hassle, low-cost additives for food, feed and personal care.

Vision: The operational excellence leader in additives and additive expertise for the food, feed and personal care industries.

Strategic imperatives

◆ Operational excellence:
  - *Reliable, no-hassle and speedy customer service and product supply;*
  - *Simplification and cost reductions in manufacturing and overhead;*
  - *Selective and cost-efficient technical support;*
  - *R&D focused on manufacturing efficiency and large-volume products.*

◆ Focus on growth in vitamins, colours, sweeteners, anti-oxidants and blends:
  - Expand sweetener customer base;
  - Protect sales in personal care, colours and feed.

◆ Globalize. Increase sales in Asia Pacific and build cheaper, local manufacturing.

SUMMARY

To recap, here's how to turn all these ingredients into a coherent strategy:

1. Describe who you are today, using 80/20 segment analysis, customer feedback and the value discipline, and the definition of your competences.

2. Categorize your segments in three categories defined initially just by profitability – 'Expand aggressively', 'Maintain', 'Harvest' or 'Exit'.

3. Validate and refine the categorization based on your competitive position, business attractiveness and the fit with your competences.

4. Based on your 'A' segments and your value discipline, write a succinct mission and vision, and three to five strategic imperatives.

11

HOW TO RAISE PROFITS QUICKLY

Strategy determines your fundamental direction in the coming years. Now it is time to act on it and use it for short-term improvement.

Short-term profit improvement is almost always possible by reducing costs and focusing on fewer segments, where your company has a clear competitive advantage. It may also be possible to push through some tactical price increases, particularly if the product or service can be improved.

Jack pays full attention for once!

I had reached the point where I felt sure of Jack's full attention, so much so that while in the office, he did not want to be disturbed unless matters were absolutely urgent. 'I'm going to summarize what we have learnt so far, and then outline how I feel you should proceed to increase profits,' I told him. I used an overhead projector and put up a few slides covering the following points.

Diagnosis: UTC's position

1. UTC is in ten market segments, each of which requires a different approach.

2. UTC makes 85 per cent of its profits in the US branded tea business, which represents 40 per cent of sales. UTC is the market leader, a third

larger than United Foods. The segment is low growth and UTC is losing share to United Foods. It is an attractive business to be in.

3. The supermarkets' most important purchase criteria are price and brand strength, with service and packaging also important. UTC scores better than United Foods on all criteria, with the important exception of price. United Foods prices its tea to consumers 5 per cent below UTC's prices and also gives the supermarkets 2 per cent more margin than UTC. Price is the only reason why United Foods is gaining market share from UTC.

4. United Foods has 5 per cent lower costs in producing and selling its tea than UTC. Given UTC's greater scale, equal efficiency would lead to UTC having costs 7 per cent lower than today.

5. US herb tea comprises less than 7 per cent of UTC's sales but is responsible for 37 per cent of its profits (the reason that US branded tea and US herb tea provide over 100 per cent of current UTC profits is because of losses in private label). This is a highly attractive market, with 15 per cent market growth annually. UTC is a clear market leader, and enjoys a return on sales in this business of a staggering 14 per cent, but is losing market share quite fast to Herbal Health.

6. The most important purchase criteria in herb teas are brand and product innovation, closely followed by packaging, price and service. UTC performs better than Herbal Health on all criteria except price, where it is significantly less competitive, since Herbal Health prices 5 per cent lower.

7. Herbal Health has roughly equal costs to UTC, which, taking into account UTC's advantage of being nearly three times larger, suggests there is an opportunity to lower UTC costs by 4 per cent.

8. Herbal tea is a 'star' business, where market share must be defended for the sake of long-term profits and cash flow. If UTC priced 4–5 per cent lower than today, to roughly match Herbal Health prices, it is unlikely that Herbal Health would reduce its prices. If this is correct, UTC could reverse the loss of market share and consolidate its leadership position.

9. The US fruit tea business contributes less than 3 per cent of UTC revenues but provides more than 13 per cent of profits. Its characteristics are almost identical to those of herb tea, though the leading competitor (Fruit-Tea Fun) is different. This is another star business where UTC is losing valuable market share through pricing too high.

10. The export markets for branded tea generate 15 per cent of revenues but 40 per cent of profits. UTC is gaining market share in all major export markets, but is only the leader in rest of the world (that is, markets other than North America and Europe), which mainly means positions of strength in Asia. The rest of the world branded tea business is highly profitable and well run.

11. The herb and fruit tea export markets are very small, but profitable and growing fast. UTC is in weak but improving market share positions. Profits may be vulnerable if market prices fall, but it is worthwhile trying to attain leadership positions, particularly if this can be done by acquisition.

12. By far the biggest UTC problem, and by far the biggest opportunity, lies in the US private label tea business. The losses on the contract with Big Boy Supermarkets comes to $18m, or 86 per cent of the net level of profits. Yet this is an attractive business to be in, with few suppliers and a high average level of profitability (UTC is the only player losing money in it). UTC has a reasonable market share position.

13. The unbranded market has surprising purchase criteria, with the most important being product innovation and willingness to provide new and unique products under the supermarkets' brands. Price is also important. Packaging is not. UTC is rated well on price (as is Cheapco, the largest competitor), but performs poorly on product innovation and offering proprietary products to the supermarkets. It is important to note, however, that Cheapco performs even worse, and significantly worse, than UTC on these two most important criteria.

14. Cheapco has costs 10 per cent lower than UTC in unbranded tea, of which 3 per cent relates to cheaper packaging. There appears to be an opportunity to move the general level of prices up.

15. The most important opportunity for UTC in unbranded tea, besides lowering costs, lies in providing proprietary product to the chains. This could lead to large and profitable new business, since price sensitivity on unique product is lower and the volumes could be very large, without any need for expensive advertising.

As I went through the list, Jack was uncharacteristically silent and attentive. At the end, he asked simply, 'But what do I do?' This was the perfect cue for my next slide:

Five recommendations to Jack

1. In US branded tea, cut list prices by 2 per cent and offer another 2 per cent additional margin to the supermarkets, in order to stop market share loss.

2. Cut costs in US branded tea by 7 per cent within two years.

3. In US herb and fruit teas, cut prices by 4–5 per cent to reverse the market share loss. Reduce costs by 4 per cent within 18 months.

4. In the US unbranded tea market, raise prices by 2 per cent immediately, and cut costs by a total of 10 per cent over two years, 3 per cent of which (relating to packaging) can be done immediately.

5. Mount a campaign to provide leading retailers (especially Big Boy) with unique new products to be sold under their own house brands. Target revenues of $100m by the end of year one and $250m by the end of year two.

I then moved on to a final slide, shown as Illustration 2.65, summarizing the potential effect on profit:

ILLUSTRATION 2.65

Potential effect on operating profit of recommendations to UTC ($m)

	Year 1	Year 2	Year 3
1. US Branded Tea 4% price cut	(8.0)	(8.0)	(8.0)
2. US Branded Tea new volume	0.8	2.0	4.4
3. US Branded Tea cost cutting	3.7	7.3	12.8
4. US Fruit and Herb Tea 4–5% price cut	(3.5)	(4.1)	(4.7)
5. US Fruit and Herb Tea new volume	0.9	2.1	3.5
6. US Fruit and Herb Tea cost cutting	1.1	2.4	2.7
7. US Private Label Tea 2% price rise	7.8	7.8	7.8
8. US Private Label Tea cost cutting	12.0	24.1	40.2
9. US Private Label Tea unique new products	1.5	8.8	12.5
Net change	16.3	42.4	71.2
Previous budget	22.0	24.2	26.6
Total profit	38.3	66.6	97.8
Total revenues after new initiatives	950	1265	1370
Implied return on sales	4.0%	5.3%	7.1%

The implied return on sales is calculated as a reality check. In this type of business, successful competitors make 10 per cent return on sales, but anything above that is generally not sustainable. Although I estimated that Jack had the potential to increase his operating profits to more than 450 per cent of today's level, the third year return on sales, at just over 7 per cent, still looks reasonable.

In the UTC example, Richard showed how to improve profit based purely on business segment information. If you undertook a 'business fingerprint' as explained in Chapter 3, then there are two additional ways to tackle profit improvement.

The first is 80/20 product analysis. As with all such analysis, the objective is to identify which products are critical, and conversely, which are not.

We could also use 80/20 analysis to identify critical customers. But even more useful is a WHITNEY ANALYSIS, which doesn't just consider the profitability of your customers, but also their size and strategic importance.

Size and strategic importance matter. Losing a large customer is a much bigger headache than losing a few small ones. Strategic customers are those that provide long-term growth, where you are better at serving them than competitors.

Customers are scored on each category, and classified according to the matrix in Illustration 2.66. The classification serves to determine how each customer class is served, and what improvement actions are taken. To a large extent these are guided by your value discipline.

ILLUSTRATION 2.66
Customer classification matrix

Strategic	Large	Profitable	Class
Yes	Yes	Yes	A
Yes	No	Yes	A
Yes	Yes	No	B
Yes	No	No	B
No	Yes	Yes	B
No	Yes	No	C
No	No	Yes	D
No	No	No	D

Addit evaluates products and customers

'OK,' said Hank, looking over the vision, mission and strategy: 'We have to focus, we have to lower costs and we have to build a plant in Asia. That last part is easy, but how do we go about the rest?'

I found the plant remark amusing, but kept a straight face. 'Well,' I replied, first we need to set growth targets for the sales people, making sure they focus on the A segments. Probably they should get bigger bonuses and higher pay rises if they hit the sales targets on the A segments.

'But,' I continued, 'I do think we need to know more to be able to cut costs intelligently.'

I knew all too well how companies go about cutting costs. When profits drop below a critical level, all hell breaks loose and costs are taken out indiscriminately. Profit contributors are hit as hard as loss-makers. A bad situation is often made worse.

Addit's analyst showed some facts about Addit's product profitability (Illustration 2.67). 'Here you see each of your five hundred or so products. Each dot represents a product's net sales and corresponding profit. They are sorted by decreasing return on sales, and then each of sales and profit are plotted cumulatively.'

ILLUSTRATION 2.67

Analysis of Addit products' cumulative sales and profit

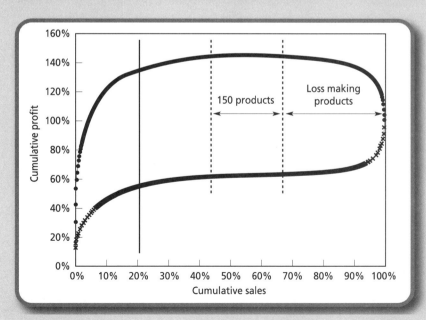

'The left-hand side of the curve shows your most profitable products. Note that 20 per cent of the products, about one hundred in total, generates almost 55 per cent of sales, and 135 per cent of profits.'

'On the right of the graph there's a tail of loss-making products. Some of them are high volume. You need to fix that.'

'Finally, in the middle of the graph are some one hundred and fifty products that hardly add sales or profit.'

Hank, the US marketing manager, asked: 'You're not saying that we should sell just those one hundred on the left, and stop selling the other four hundred, are you? Don't forget that those products cover a lot of costs. Without them we wouldn't make that 135 per cent of profit!'

Hank was right. Even if a product makes a loss, it usually covers some over-heads. Cut the loss-making product without cutting the overheads and the loss will go through the roof. But this is really a short-term/long-term issue. In the long-term it makes no sense to sell products at a loss – it is far better either to remove the overhead, or use it to support profitable products. There will always be a heated debate about this issue, and today was no exception![4]

I decided to stir it up a little. 'Hank,' I said with an enigmatic smile, 'I think it's worse than that, or rather we need to be more extreme than selling a hundred products. How about selling just nine of them?'

My shock tactics led to silence. I put up a second graph, where, as before, each dot represents a product's net sales and corresponding profit. But now they are sorted by decreasing absolute profit, then plotted cumulatively (Illustration 2.68).

'Just nine products generate 84 per cent of the profit. Can you imagine how simple and profitable Addit would be if it focused on those nine, putting all the effort into selling them and perhaps doubling or tripling their sales? That's less than 2 per cent of the total product portfolio! If you tripled the sales of those nine products and did nothing else, you'd be working a great deal less than you do today and be making two-and-a-half times as much profit, even with all the overheads!'

The group was stunned. I added that twenty-two products make a full 100 per cent of Addit's profit today, on fewer than 40 per cent of the sales.

'Now to answer Hank properly, of course, Addit can't just stop selling four hundred and ninety products...'

'... but you need to realize that Addit is a complex operation, making and selling five hundred products. There's a reason your products are expensive, and this is it.'[5]

---

[4] See the section on INCREMENTAL SALES in the Glossary.
[5] See the sections on COST OF COMPLEXITY and AVERAGE COSTING in the Glossary.

ILLUSTRATION 2.68

Addit's products plotted by decreasing absolute profit

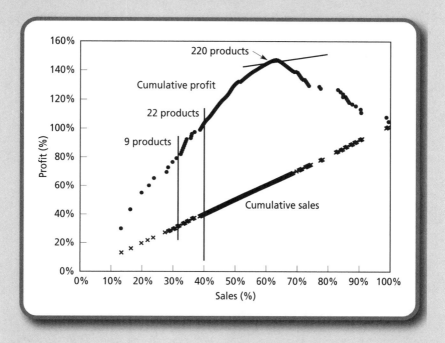

'On top of that, customers say they don't value a broad product portfolio.'

'Have a look at this mountain top, where your profit peaks and then starts dropping,' – I pointed at the graph – 'it includes two hundred and twenty low-volume products. Together they have sales of £11.5 million and make a loss of £150,000. They are prime targets for elimination.'

'I bet you can cut half of the five hundred products – in a smart way, shifting customers to other, more profitable, products. You'd slash complexity, so reducing costs and becoming even more profitable and competitive in the most important products.'

'This complexity appears not only in your products, but also in your customer portfolio. Remember Whitney and how last week we went through the customer list to determine strategic customers? Here's the result of that exercise.' (See Illustration 2.69.)

'Addit has about 2,000 customers. Two hundred and thirty-five of these are labelled A. These are all profitable and strategic, all in the most important segments, and important for the long term. These customers need to be cuddled, and Addit must constantly increase its share of their business. You know how to

ILLUSTRATION 2.69

Addit's customer classification

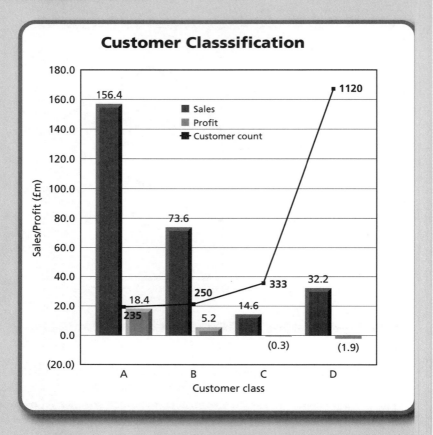

do that: OE, operational excellence. Providing no-hassle service, reliability in product quality and delivery, and a better price.'

'There are slightly more customers in the B category. Most of them are strategic. Some are large. Not all are profitable.'

'In the C category are the non-strategic, but large customers. They make a loss, but fill the plants. Under OE you want to keep them, but not at all costs. In any case, minimize costs to serve them.'

'Last come the D customers. They're all small and non-strategic. Some make a profit but overall these 1,120 customers – 60 per cent of the total – make a loss.'

Sue hadn't seen the graph before. She jumped right in: 'So who do you think our people in sales and customer service are most busy with?'

Emphatically circling the '1,120' number, she answered her own question: 'It's clear – with the D customers! There are lots of them and they're probably more expensive because of all the smaller volumes and packages they order.'

Sue circled the A customer bars: 'Meanwhile we can't serve our A and B customers, who make the real money.' Some of the marketing managers grumbled that this was not true, but Sue was not listening. 'Guys, we have to do something. Should we hike prices to these D customers?'

I stepped back in: 'Sue, that's why we're doing this, to find out how to best deal with each group. Each has a certain value for your business; and each has to be served in a specific way. How exactly depends on your value discipline.'

'Now, you've chosen OE, that's all about supply chain and efficiency. Specifically, reliable logistics, smooth ordering and a lower price. The point is, can you offer that to D customers?'

Jake, the manufacturing manager, reacted: 'Do we even want to?' Jake never said much, but when he did, people listened. 'I mean, in manufacturing we are not terribly good at serving them. It's a lot of hassle, all those small packages. Our people don't like it, they're not proud about it. We may not like to hear that, but it's true. Big volume goes much better. And our salespeople are not good at getting the right price. Maybe the D customers are just not for us.'

'I think you hit the nail on the head,' I said. 'Serving small customers is a distinct skill, some are better at it than others. Addit needs large volume and standardization to keep the price low. Dealing with small customers, small volumes, and their special needs just doesn't fit – which is why you lose money.'

'But that would mean we would outsource more than half of our customer base!' said Hank.

'Exactly' replied Sue, 'and that's just what's going to happen. I'm not prepared to subsidize these customers and make everyone work like crazy for it. Let's turn them over to our distributors.'

'Sue,' I said 'I think that's a great idea. You can sell large volumes to your distributors, and they can break it up in smaller packaging. You may need to give them some price support, but if you move carefully even that may not be necessary.'

'But what if the customers don't accept that?' Hank asked. 'What if they stop buying from us? Some of them are profitable and it's £32 million sales.

Paul, the European marketing manager, reached out: 'Hank, let's work on this together. I've done this in my former job, and you know what, we only lost a handful of customers. Instead, we doubled sales to distributors in two years!'

Hank raised his eyebrows, but then smiled and said: 'I guess it can't hurt to give it a go.'

I smiled too. 'Great. Now let's finish up with a few actions,' I said. Turning to the marketing managers: 'Tell me if we can do these five things please:

'First, can we decide how we want to service the A, B, and C customers, giving most attention to the As and least to the Cs?

'Second, can we evaluate all loss-making customers? Why is each one unprofitable? It could be due to price, or manufacturing costs, or service costs. Make specific plans to increase price or reduce costs.

'Third, aim to transfer D customers to distributors? Develop partnerships with them. It would free up a lot of your resources.

'Fourth, can we look at the small-volume products and see if we can shed them? Can customers be convinced to take another, similar product? We could probably aim to halve the product range within two years.

'Finally, among the remaining products, can we look at the big-volume loss-makers? Can we raise price? Reduce costs? If nothing works, consider dropping them? Can we have this done within twelve months?'

The guys were nodding. They could see a brighter future, based on giving the really profitable customers more reasons to buy more from Addit, and finding new customers like them.

Improvement actions for Addit

1. Reduce overall manufacturing costs by 5 per cent a year for three years, through:
   a. transferring D customers to distributors, with retention of sales;
   b. reducing product portfolio by at least half;
   c. moving production to a cheaper plant in Asia.

2. Freeze selling, administration, and research costs in the first year, then allow them to increase annually at a rate below sales growth. Focus R&D on supporting the strategy and stop extraneous work.

3. Gain market share in 'grow aggressively' segments, expanding at least twice as fast as the market. Focus especially on Asia. Grow even faster in new extracts, anti-oxidants, and sweeteners. Carefully reduce sales to integrated feed manufacturers and replace by sales to pre-mixers.

4. Cut prices in personal care and anti-oxidants by 5 per cent in a year. Hold all other prices so they drop in real terms to support sales growth

5. Lower raw material costs in personal care, pet food and anti-oxidants by 2.5 per cent in the first and second years.

Addit's managers were asked to submit department plans along these lines.

Taken together, these actions – which are neither extraordinary nor particularly aggressive – would reduce Addit's manufacturing costs from their current high level of 19.1 per cent to an acceptable 14.6 per cent of sales. Selling, admin and research costs would drop from over 14 per cent to just above 13 per cent.

These actions would double Addit's profit within three years and increase return on sales to 14.3 per cent (Illustration 2.70). The industry average of 15.5 per cent acted as a reality check, indicating that the profit improvement plan was reasonable.

The strategy worked well. Addit grew its sweetener sales by 20 per cent a year, beating the 15 per cent target. Sales in Asia doubled, far better than planned. The transfer of D customers was a huge success. Very few customers were lost and the distributors reached even more of them, doubling sales to their target customer group. Absolute profits, after five years, had gone up by two-and-a-half times.

ILLUSTRATION 2.70

Potential effect of Addit's three-year improvement plan ($m)

Code	Segment	Market growth	Target growth	Year 0 NS (£m)	Year 0 Profit (£m)	Year 1 NS (£m)	Year 1 Profit (£m)	Year 2 NS (£m)	Year 2 Profit (£m)	Year 3 NS (£m)	Year 3 Profit (£m)
1000	Animal nutrition	3.3%	3.5%	48.3	3.5	50.0	4.9	51.7	5.7	53.5	6.5
2000	Human nutrition	4.4%	8.3%	107.1	10.3	115.8	14.8	125.7	19.0	136.7	23.8
2100	Vitamins	4.0%	8.0%	42.6	8.4	46.0	10.3	49.7	11.8	53.7	13.3
2200	Colors	4.0%	4.0%	30.4	4.3	31.6	5.1	32.8	5.6	34.2	6.2
2300	Anti-oxidants	2.0%	7.5%	4.0	(0.5)	4.1	(0.3)	4.4	(0.2)	4.7	(0.0)
2400	Sweeteners	7.5%	15.0%	18.8	(1.4)	21.6	(0.1)	24.9	1.5	28.6	3.3
2500	New extracts	4.0%	20.0%	5.2	(1.2)	6.2	(0.8)	7.5	(0.5)	9.0	0.2
2600	Other human nutrition	2.0%	2.0%	6.2	0.6	6.3	0.7	6.4	0.8	6.5	0.8
3000	**Personal care**	3.5%	3.5%	25.6	0.9	25.2	5.1	26.0	1.9	27.0	2.2
4000	**Nutritional blends**	2.5%	5.0%	20.8	4.2	21.8	5.1	22.9	5.8	24.1	6.5
5000	**Other**	2.9%	1.4%	75.1	2.4	76.1	4.4	77.3	5.6	77.5	6.6
	Total			276.9	21.4	288.9	34.2	303.7	38.0	318.7	45.6
	ROS				7.7%		11.8%		12.5%		14.3%

SUMMARY

In summary, short-term improvements can be achieved by:

1. Taking actions at the segment level, through changing the priorities of segments, focusing on the most profitable ones and putting much effort into winning extra business here, harvesting weak ones and getting out of loss-makers.

2. Using 80/20 and Whitney analyses to take targeted actions for particular customers and products.

12

CONCLUSION

So much for UTC and Addit, which are disguised real-life businesses that did make these profit improvements from their new strategies.

We've now reached the end of our step-by-step guide on business strategy. We hope you agree:

◆ *Strategy is fun!*

◆ *Strategy is easy!*

Strategy makes sense of what you do day-to-day. Strategy is the way to make your business:

◆ *More and more different from any other business.*

◆ *Better and better at serving your best, most profitable customers.*

◆ *A rewarding business for you to run and/or own.*

If you've enjoyed this strategy journey and found it useful – and how could this not be the case?! – please tell your colleagues and friends to use this approach.

But don't breathe a word to your competitors!

PART THREE

HINTS ON MANAGING THE STRATEGY PROCESS

13

SELLING THE NEED FOR A NEW STRATEGY

As head of a business, your first objective, before undertaking a strategic review, may be to sell the *need* for it – to your own executives, or to your boss, head office, or the owners.

If your business is in bad shape, this may not be hard. People up and down the organization will have a sense of urgency and expect you to do something. In fact, your main challenge may be to avoid premature action, before your analysis is completed.

It may be more difficult to sell the need for a strategy when the business appears to be doing well. But meeting targets does not mean that there are no bumps in the road ahead, or that you're doing as well as you could. That's why private equity houses are often better owners than many corporations. Private equity partners give executives great incentives to run the business at full stretch.

Here are some rationales for undertaking a strategic review. At least some of them are likely to apply to your position and can be used to justify the review:

◆ *A strategy has not been developed or updated in more than five years. While certain individuals may have the right insights, the business as a whole is probably unaware of its strengths and weaknesses, or of critical issues it's facing.*

◆ *Profitability is slipping – and no-one knows precisely why or how to restore it.*

◆ *Profitability is below shareholders' required rate of return.*

◆ *While total performance is acceptable, executives don't know which areas are the most profitable, or disagree on this.*

◆ *The business has a broad portfolio of customers and/or products, many of which are small-volume. This implies complexity – which may be obscuring the big picture.*

◆ *Growth is lacklustre and there is an air of complacency. The business is coasting and needs to be revitalized with clear insights and objectives.*

◆ *The business is investing in blue sky 'innovation' or 'diversification' projects outside of its core business and they don't seem to be bearing fruit.*

◆ *Shifts are evident in the marketplace, but there's no consensus on how important they are or how the business should react to them.*

◆ *New competitors are making inroads, or new products are coming into the market.*

Let's assume there are some of these tell-tale signs showing the need for a new strategy. But what are the tangible benefits that the strategy could provide to your bosses? Why should they want to spend time and money on strategy?

First, because it's very profitable. Typically, a good new strategy will improve profits by between 50 per cent and 500 per cent within three to five years. We've seen such improvements in many different industries, with many different teams of managers and in different business cycles. Your business won't be different.

Second, if your business is part of a corporate portfolio, the strategy can create value beyond your own business. Knowing your competitive positions, value discipline, industry attractiveness and competencies, the centre can assess the fit of your business within the corporation. The centre can then decide to what extent the corporation is a good parent for the business and can aid in the development of the business. If there is not a good fit, then both the centre and the business are better off by separating. If there is a good fit, then the centre can help exploit your competencies and strengths across the corporation. Conversely, it can contribute to developing the business by linking with skills available elsewhere in the corporation.

Finally, the process will train your managers in strategy. They will experience how strategy is developed and applied, and how it can deliver results. This will be valuable for the firm as well as the individuals.

MANAGING THE PROJECT

Someone needs to be in charge: the 'sponsor' – probably the chief executive, unit head, business manager, or owner.

Next you'll need a project leader working closely with the sponsor to organize meetings, set objectives, request inputs, send out meeting agendas, and so on. If you're following the top-down approach (as Richard did with UTC), this person can also take care of data gathering and analysis. If you are following the bottom-up approach, you'll need someone dedicated to that, for example a business analyst.

Finally, decide whom to involve in the strategy development process. Include anyone who will be important in realizing the new strategy.

How long will it take? A top-down strategy can be devised within four months. UTC steamed through the process within two months, but in a true do–it–yourself setting that may be hard to achieve. In particular the customer survey can take some time to prepare and carry out. All the other elements are in your own hands so you can set the pace.

The more thorough bottom-up approach will take between three and twelve months. Addit took a year, giving ample opportunity for its executives to contribute while still taking care of day-to-day business. Two- or three-day meetings were organized every five or six weeks. The first six meetings were all about gathering data, followed by two dedicated to data evaluation, and one to hammer out the strategy and an implementation plan. The process should not last more than a year, to avoid exhaustion or staleness.

Would outside consultants speed the process? Yes. But don't be fooled. As the consultants are working away, there's the risk that your executives may not be properly involved. When the consultants turn over their work to be implemented, you will have to take time to sell their conclusions. This process can take significant time, and sometimes doesn't succeed at all.

That's where our approach scores. It puts you and your managers in the lead. So when the strategy is done, you get straight to work. The do-it-yourself approach is cheaper, creates better and faster buy-in, and develops your people's abilities. It is also more rewarding and, quite simply, fun.

While we have written our book to be a do-it-yourself guide, the involvement of Richard and Peter in the UTC and Addit cases shows how it can be helpful to involve someone with experience. If you'd prefer this, contact us at *www.simplystrategy.com*. We'll put you in touch with a high-quality facilitator to provide expert know-how and pace the process.

'PROGRESSIVE APPROXIMATION'

While you go through the ten steps of strategy development, there will be questions that need to be answered. For example, you will need to know the market share of your competitors in your newly defined business segment. Or something on industry attractiveness. Or even another strategy-related question, not explicitly dealt with in our ten steps. A great deal of time can be wasted on trying to get precise and definite answers. Very often the worst result is not the waste of time, but exhaustion or impatience on the part of the participants, which leads them to conclude that strategic thinking is too academic, wearisome or 'anti-action' to be of any use to them. The answer to this syndrome is 'progressive approximation'.

The basic point of progressive approximation is that you should come up with your best initial answer very quickly, and then decide whether it is worth the time and effort to improve on it by doing additional data-gathering and analysis. This, in fact, is how most of us go about our daily lives – although we may not recognize it as such – and we see no reason why strategy development should be different.

There is one big caution: progressive approximation should never be an excuse for managers not to challenge themselves. In our experience, many businesses have incorrect assumptions and beliefs about their business segments, customers' buying criteria and competitors. In this case strategic decisions are bound to be wrong in part or in whole. More extensive data-gathering or the use of an outside consultant can help to point out such inconsistencies and to stimulate discussion.

Keeping these things in mind, the procedure is:

◆ *With your team, state as clearly and crisply as you can the questions you want to answer: the critical issues. The idea is that if you knew the answers to these issues you would know exactly what to do. Do this on one sheet of paper: you should have no more than seven critical issues (ideally between four and six).*

◆ *Then construct, on another single sheet of paper, your hypotheses on the critical issues. Each hypothesis is your best guess at what the answer might be. At this stage it matters not a hoot whether you are right or wrong; the important thing is to reach consensus on a possible answer, so that you can then test your hypothesis later in the light of new information or insight.*

◆ *Now list on a third sheet the information you would ideally like to help you resolve each critical issue. When you have finished, take another page and compile two columns, labelled 'Most important data' on the left and 'Easiest-to-find data' on the right, and rank the information you want under both headings. Decide on the information you would like to acquire first: in other words, some combination of the most important and most accessible. Italicize the data you aim to collect in this first round. Decide how the data are to be acquired, who is to do this and when you will all meet again to review the results.*

◆ *Review the new data, and see whether they support or differ from your hypotheses. Does the data make clear what the strategy should be? If you are still in doubt, or there is lack of consensus, agree what the most important points still at issue are, and decide what data should be gathered in the second round to help settle the issue. Then decide who will collect the data and when you will review the results collectively.*

◆ *Continue the process until you have agreed either on the answer, or there is a consensus that the answer is likely to be X and that the cost and delay involved in further investigation is not merited, so that everyone agrees that X should be pursued.*

◆ *Document the results of this process to keep a record of what you hypothesized, what you learned in data collection, what you concluded and what you decided to do. This document should be easily accessible for periodic review by operating managers.*

This process of progressive approximation will give you a quicker, cheaper and probably better answer than conventional methods, but the main benefit is that the new strategy will be implemented more quickly and effectively. On some complex and important issues you may still need to use consultants, but do it under the control of the operating managers and do not allow consultants to usurp the process. The operating managers must remain in charge, and must do the main thinking.

STRATEGY REALIZATION

There are two keys to success:

1. SET A FEW KEY GOALS

It's all about results. For each person, set goals that you want achieved by the end of the year. Divide those up in quarterly milestones. Lay out the generic strategy goals for the company and, most importantly, for each department.

Don't set too many goals. Be realistic about what can be achieved by the business and each individual. Don't over-specify what should be achieved. You cannot plan for each contingency, and you need to rely on your people to take appropriate action, or refrain from it, in the context of the strategy.

2. MEASURE RESULTS

Remember that what gets measured gets done.

Check progress quarterly. Leaders march the business where it should go. Nobody else will. Take your eyes off the process of strategy realization and progress may stall, or the business may veer off in a different direction.

Be judicious. Ultimately each manager has to make a judgement about how well someone met a goal. Sometimes getting halfway in the face of adversity is a fantastic achievement. Other times meeting a goal in full may be poor performance, if much more could have been achieved.

Be appreciative. Most people want to do a good job and expect simple appreciation for their efforts. Your thanks will motivate, smooth out small changes of direction and bring people to a higher level of performance.

Communicate results graphically. Use easy-to-grasp charts. Nothing complicated, not too many, just simple numbers tied directly to the strategy goals: Need to reduce manufacturing costs? Measure average production unit costs monthly to see whether they are going down. Improve sales in segment XYZ? Measure that. Increase manufacturing reliability? Track mistakes. Use the charts in your quarterly discussions, and encourage your managers to do the same in their discussions with their staff.

NOW START YOUR OWN ADVENTURE ...

We've now reached the end of our guide to business strategy. We hope you've found it simple and refreshing, and can see how it can help your business become much more focused, much more fun and much more profitable. You're in the thick of the daily battle. Surely now you realize that you can tilt the playing field in your favour through a simple new strategy. With the right strategy, life is far more rewarding, yet far easier too. If your strategy doesn't do this for you, then you've got the wrong strategy!

Good luck, and enjoy the adventure, as many thousands who've used these tools have already done. We're counting on you!

STRATEGY AND ITS HISTORY

A BRIEF HISTORY OF STRATEGY

The beginnings of business strategy can be traced back at least as far as Alfred Chandler, who was active and influential from the late 1950s. His 1962 book, *Strategy and Structure*, states that corporations should develop their strategy before deciding their (organizational) structure – form should follow purpose. Arguably, the roots of strategy go back much further, for example to Alfred Sloan's reorganization of General Motors in 1921 (though this was documented only in *My Years with General Motors*, not published until 1963).

Some say that Peter Drucker set the ball rolling much earlier. His 1946 book, *Concepts of the Corporation*, looked at General Motors, as well as General Electric, IBM and Sears Roebuck. Drucker said the most successful companies were centralized and good at setting goals. He was the first to see that the purpose of a business was external, that is, in creating and satisfying customer needs.

Whether 'strategy' began in 1921, 1946 or later, it definitely grew to powerful adolescence in the 1960s. The first half of the decade saw a new focus on strategy in academic quarters. In 1960, Theodore Levitt wrote 'Marketing Myopia' in the *Harvard Business Review*, a pioneering attempt to look at corporate strategy from a radical and broad perspective; the article has since sold more than half a million reprinted copies. In 1965 came the bible of strategic planning, H. Igor Ansoff's monumental *Corporate Strategy*, a thoughtful and incredibly detailed blueprint for planning a firm's objectives, expansion plan, product-market positions and resource allocation. The effects of this book – by no means all benign – cannot be underestimated. It framed the mindset of a whole generation of managers and lead to the creation of elaborate corporate strategy departments, whose advent and merciful demise have given a bad name to 'strategic planning'. Even today, many managers harbor a conscious or unconscious antipathy to strategy, due to past corporate center strategic interference that appeared too convoluted and irrelevant to be of any practical help to operating businesses.

But perhaps the most important development strategy was the founding in 1964 of the Boston Consulting Group (BCG) by Bruce Henderson. Starting with 'one room, one person, one desk, and no secretary', by the end of the decade Henderson had built a powerful machine combining intellectual innovation and boardroom consulting, and had invented both the EXPERIENCE CURVE and the GROWTH/SHARE MATRIX, probably the two most powerful tools in strategy. More generally, BCG blended market analysis and research together with financial theory to produce the micro-economic analysis of competitors and their relative costs that is the bedrock of all subsequent strategy. BCG's period of maximum intellectual creativity and invention can be traced fairly precisely to the years 1967–1973.

Intellectual development, though possibly at a more muted pace, has continued since. Perhaps the landmark books of the 1970s were *The Nature of Managerial Work* (1973) by Henry Mintzberg, and *Strategic Management* (1979) by H. Igor Ansoff.

The 1980s saw the emergence of two other writers who have influenced and deepened our view of strategy: Michael Porter and Kenich Ohmae. Porter, a Harvard academic, shot to fame with his celebrated 1980 title, *Competitive Advantage: Techniques for Analyzing Industries and Competitors*. Porter argued that the profitability of corporations was determined not only by a firm's relative competitive position (as Henderson had proved), but also by the structural characteristics of the firm's industry, which could be described in clear, micro-economic terms.

Ohmae, a cosmopolitan Japanese, described quite brilliantly how Japanese companies had benefited by using strategy (though largely without strategy consultants or Western academics). His 1982 book, *The Mind of the Strategist: The art of Japanese business* is compulsive reading and still one of the best explanations of how strategy is most effective when it combines analysis, intuition and willpower in the pursuit of global dominance.

Over the past decade or so, important contributions to strategic thinking have been made by Gary Hamel and C. K. Prahalad, by John Kay, and by a trio of writers from the Ashridge Strategic Management Center - Andrew Campbell, Michael Goold and Marcus Alexander.

In 1989, Gary Hamel and C.K. Prahalad broke new ground with an article entitled 'Strategic intent'. They argued that successful companies had ambitions out of all proportion to their positions and had a commitment to change the rules of the game. The following year, Prahalad and Hamel argued in another article, 'The core competence of the corporation', and later in a book with a similar title, that the key to strategy was a firm's distinctive skills, technologies and assets, and its collective learning ability. Professor Kay and others have elaborated on this 'resource-based' view of strategy – that the resources a firm enjoys, its people and knowledge, are more important than its market positions.

Michel Robert, a persuasive advocate of the resource view, asserted that the most successful companies are those that leverage their unique set of competencies across their business units. Robert pointed to telling examples such as Honda – with a core competency in engines – and Hewlett Packard – in instrumentation technology. There followed a frenzy of core competency navel-gazing.

Corporate strategy was greatly deepened in 1994 by the publication of *Corporate-Level Strategy* by Goold, Campbell and Alexander. They argued that the corporate center should be seen as a 'parent' and develop 'parenting skills' to help its operating companies, and that unless the center comprised the best possible parent for each business, it should be divested.

In 1995, Treacy and Wiersema elaborated a concept put forward earlier by Porter, namely that of the VALUE DISCIPLINE. In *The Discipline of Market Leaders*, they said that companies succeed through relentless pursuit of *one* particular characteristic appreciated by customers. Businesses should choose one of the three value disciplines:

◆ *Operational excellence: offering ease of purchase and use at a low price.*

◆ *Customer intimacy: providing a tailored solution for each customer.*

◆ *Product leadership: providing leading edge products and services.*

SWINGS IN STRATEGIC THINKING – SIX PHASES

PHASE 1: PLANNING FOR LARGE, MULTI-PRODUCT FIRMS (1950s–1960s)

The first focus, at the end of the 1950s and in the 1960s, was on the best way to plan the development of large, multi-product firms. This was the province of classic strategic planning at the center, although the dominant prescription was to decentralize into largely autonomous divisions and to diversify by making acquisitions in attractive but often unrelated businesses.

PHASE 2: PORTFOLIO MANAGEMENT (1965–1975)

The second, and most fruitful, period was dominated by BCG's concept of portfolio management. BCG's micro-economic approach was highly prescriptive, telling firms to:

◆ *focus on business positions where the firm had, or could realistically obtain, market leadership and divest other businesses;*

◆ *focus on cash rather than profit;*

◆ *aim for cost advantage over competitors (i.e. have lower costs than them);*

◆ *manage competitors so they would withdraw from the firm's main profit segments;*

◆ *use debt aggressively to finance growth, reinforce market leadership and raise returns for stockholders;*

◆ *avoid over-extending the product line or building in too much complexity or overhead;*

◆ *use excess cash flow to diversify and apply the precepts of portfolio management to a new set of businesses.*

BCG's ideas encouraged two already established and related trends – towards building up large central planning departments in conglomerates, and towards further diversification. Neither of these was central to BCG's world-view, yet both came back to haunt strategists later.

PHASE 3: 'STRATEGY PLANNING' RETREAT (early 1970s)

The third phase, the mid-to late 1970s, was one of intellectual exhaustion, corporate disillusion and a retreat into pragmatism on the part of the strategists. By now it was clear that the micro-economic techniques for analyzing competitive advantage were very powerful. They were increasingly used, however, not at the level of central, corporate strategy, but for developing business unit strategy. This was partly because the earlier promise of central portfolio management became increasingly discredited. After the oil price shock of 1973 and the stock market crash of 1974, which hit go-go conglomerates particularly hard, the virtues of both central planning and conglomerate diversification became tarnished. Furthermore, firms like GE and Siemens that had established huge central strategic planning departments soon found the results from these bureaucratic behemoths profoundly disappointing. Intellectually, the GROWTH/SHARE MATRIX, the icon of portfolio management, came under sustained attack. The assault was largely misconceived, but BCG chose discretion rather than valor. The BCG matrix went largely undefended; it became unfairly neglected.

PHASE 4: THE CREATIVE ASPECTS (from mid–1970s)

The fourth strand in strategic thinking, stretching from 1973 to the present, was a mild dose of heresy, a wave of reaction to the excessively analytical orientation of the BCG school. It involved a realization that firms generally did not derive their strategies scientifically and rigorously, and a celebration of the intuitive, adaptive and creative aspects of strategy.

In 1973, Henry Mintzberg challenged accepted thinking in *The Nature of Managerial Work*, pointing out that successful chief executives were intuitive action men, not reflective planners, that they cherished soft information and anecdotes rather than hard facts and figures, and that they read and wrote little, preferring face-to-face communication and decision-making. Mintzberg has since developed the idea of 'crafting strategy' using the creative, right-hand side of the brain, rather than the logical left side.

The 1980s brought to prominence Kenichi Ohmae's celebration of successful Japanese strategists: intuitive, creative leaders of Honda, Toyota, Matsushita and other firms, who were obsessed with establishing market leadership, beating competitors and satisfying customers. The period from 1980 to 1994 has further consolidated the ranks of the soft strategists, influential writers such as Charles Handy, Rosabeth Moss Kanter, Tom Peters, Richard Schonberger and Robert Waterman.

PHASE 5: RIGOROUS MICRO-ECONOMIC ANALYSIS (from 1980s)

The 1980s also saw the fifth development – the elaboration of rigorous micro-economic analysis by Michael Porter. He extended the BCG framework of competitive advantage to include structural industry factors like the threat from new entrants, the bargaining power of customers and suppliers, and the threat from substitutes. His message, though based on additional data and analyses, was similar to that of BCG from the start – the firm should try to find markets and niches where it could dominate and erect barriers against competition, either by low cost or by product/service differentiation. This message was later reinforced by Treacy and Wiersema. Porter also created a theory of national competitive advantage to overlay or underpin the micro-economic analysis of an individual firm's competitive advantage.

PHASE 6: SKILLS, LEARNING AND PURPOSE (from 1990s)

The sixth trend has been a new focus on a firm's skills and capabilities (its CORE COMPETENCIES), its ambitions and commitment, its ability to learn, its purpose, expressed at its MISSION and VISION, and on the role of the center as the PARENT of its operating businesses. Corporate strategy is seen less as overseeing the allocation of resources, and more as the definition, creation, stimulation and reinforcement of ambitious skills and capabilities that can be applied across several market segments.

It may also be worth alluding to the parallels drawn from traditional works on military strategy, such as Sun Tzu's *The Art of War*, or Von Clausewitz's *On War*. While these books can bring insight into human psychology and leadership, their relevance to strategy is dubious. Managers would do better to avoid confrontation with adversaries altogether, by creating space for innovation and winning new customers.

That said, one take-away from military experience has enormous value. Von Moltke observed that no matter how detailed a plan, eventually it has to give way, in the heat of the battle, to the judgement of frontline officers making snap decisions. The battle plan must always be complemented by the instincts of the leaders. Similarly, a good strategy should give managers the general direction and focus, while remaining open-ended and not over-planned. People are more valuable than plans – another reason why strategy should be developed by executives, not by outsiders.

These six phases represent more a progressive enriching of strategic insight, rather than a set of contradictions. There have been other influences, notably the renewed integration of strategic analysis and focus with cost reduction in the 1990s through business process re-engineering; the application of competitive data-gathering and analysis in order to value acquisition candidates; the emphasis on quality and responsiveness to customers; the importance of time-based competition, that is, getting the product to the customer as quickly as possible; a renewed focus on limiting the product line, on outsourcing and on the part of the VALUE CHAIN where the firm can have an advantage, in order to reduce the COSTS OF COMPLEXITY; and a new emphasis on organization structure as determining the ability of an organization to get close to the customer and respond appropriately. Much strategy work in the 1990s was driven by these initiatives.

At the same time, however, the work of strategists at the start of the twenty-first century is recognizably the same as that of their counterparts sixty years ago. The key is differentiating the firm from competitors and having skills and positions that no competitor can match or approach, by specializing in areas in which you have a better technology, product or service, or a lower cost position. Today, in many businesses, it may be more important to have a dominant technology or standard, which is central to unlocking value for customers, than it is to have a cost advantage based purely on scale and market share. Yet the basic idea is the same as ever – to establish and maintain a dominant position based on specialization and the ability to create value, in the area of focus, to a much larger degree than anyone else. The concepts developed by BCG in the late 1960s are as relevant as ever.

The number of strategy consultants employed by the leading strategy consulting firms grew by an astonishing 15–20 per cent a year between 1965 and

1991. The strategy consulting industry paused for breath in 1991–93 and 2000–2003, but overall has continued to grow impressively. In addition, there has been a huge increase in strategy work undertaken within client organizations by MBAs and ex-strategy consultants. Assuming that firms buying strategy consulting and employing strategists are not throwing money away, the value of strategy has increased, is increasing, and shows no sign of diminishing.

GLOSSARY OF STRATEGY TERMS

ACTIVITY-BASED COSTING (ABC)

Allocating costs to products and customers on the basis of actual activities and costs required to produce and supply those products, or serve those customers. Activity-based costing is the opposite of AVERAGE COSTING. It can simply be achieved by taking a survey of the managers and employees involved. Or costs can be tracked each day by filling out time statistics, and/or the use of technology to track where employees spend their time.

Moving from average costing to activity-based costing analysis almost always reveals that certain products or customers require much more effort and cost, whereas others require very little. The latter are found to be much more profitable than initially assumed, whereas the first are often sold at too low a price. See also the EIGHTY/TWENTY RULE and AVERAGE PRICING.

ANSOFF MATRIX

Developed by H. Igor Ansoff, a Russian-American engineer, mathematician, military strategist and operations researcher who wrote *Corporate Strategy* in 1965. The Ansoff matrix, shown in Illustration II.1, provides a framework for expanding into new areas, giving four options for innovation (or diversification), to increase sales.

Box 1, selling more of existing products in existing markets, is a low-risk strategy to gain market share. To be useful, this must specify how this objective is to be attained, for example by enlarging the sales force, increasing advertising or cutting price. Alternatively a firm might 're-invent' its existing products, basing them on a cheaper technology or including additional features at the same price.

Box 2 implies product development to sell new (or modified) products to existing customers: fine as long as the firm has a good record of product development and provided the new products share enough costs and skills with the existing products, and do not face a very strong incumbent competitor.

Box 3 takes existing products and sells them to new markets or customers. This is clearly sensible if the new markets can be cultivated at relatively little extra cost, but can be risky if a new market requires investment in fixed cost (for example, a new sales force), if the customers have different requirements

ILLUSTRATION II.1

Ansoff matrix for business development

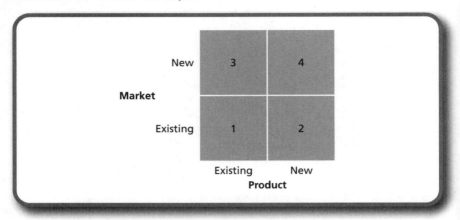

(hence don't need existing products but new or modified ones), or if there are entrenched competitors.

Box 4 – new products to new markets – is the highest risk strategy: the segments being entered are not adjacent to the existing business and it is almost like starting a new business from scratch. The presumption is that Box 4 strategies are inherently unsound and should only be taken either in desperation or because there is a compelling short-term opportunity not being exploited by others.

AVERAGE COSTING AND AVERAGE PRICING

Terms coined by the Boston Consulting Group to indicate inadequately accurate costing systems that average costs across products or services that really cause quite different amounts of cost, especially indirect and overhead costs. This can be very damaging if (as usual) it leads to average pricing, which as the name suggests means failing to charge enough of a premium for top-of-the-line or special products, and conversely charging too much for standard products (because the prices of the two types of product are averaged rather than sharply differentiated).

For example, a special or one-off product for a particular customer may cause unusual levels of cost in terms of specification, selling effort, quality control and customer liaison, yet be priced at little more than for standard products, or even at the same price. It is almost always true that traditional cost-center based methods of costing understate the cost of top-of-the-line and special products and services while overstating the cost of high-volume, standard products. The way in which average costing and pricing works is demonstrated in Illustration II.2.

Average pricing is still rife, to a much greater extent than most managers realize. They may charge more for higher specification products, but rarely enough to reflect the real (but hidden) extra cost. For example, a firm making coin mechanisms for vending machines made a special one for the London Underground system. In tendering for the business the firm put in what it considered to be a very high price, so that the managers believed the work would be highly profitable. After the contract had been completed, a consulting study using ABC analysis (ACTIVITY-BASED COSTING) showed that it had in fact been very unprofitable because of the extra time required for engineers and the additional service people needed. 'If we had understood then about average costing and average pricing,' the managers concluded, 'we would have charged 30 per cent more for the work.'

Average pricing is dangerous, not just because of losses on special products, but because it can lead to loss of market share through overpricing on the high volume, standard products. A producer who concentrates on the latter

ILLUSTRATION II.2

Average costing and pricing

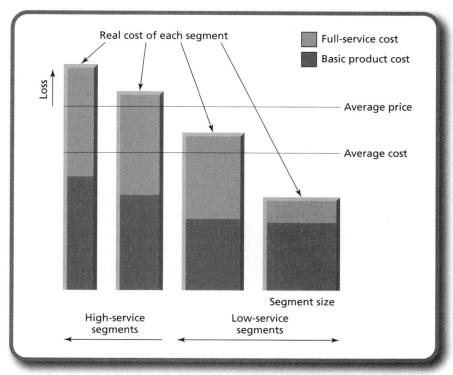

'commodity' businesses may be able to afford a much lower overhead structure, lower prices and higher profits. Over time, the specialist may gain market
share of this profitable business and leave the high-overhead, broad-line producer with a higher share of the unprofitable business. If costs are not correctly
allocated and prices set accordingly, the commercial consequences can be dire.

BARRIERS TO ENTRY

Obstacles making it difficult or impossible for competitors to enter a particular
business segment. Barriers sometimes exist naturally but astute managers will
try to raise these barriers and introduce new ones in order to restrict competition among their customers. It is worth reflecting from time to time on what
can be done to raise barriers by examining a checklist of potential barriers.

1. **Investment.** Building a bigger or better plant, service network or retail
   outlet can discourage competitors from trying to compete with you, especially if your installed customer base means it would take longer for them
   to get the scale of business to cover the cost of the initial investment, or if
   your investment gives you a lower cost base than existing competitors.

2. **Branding.** Making your product or service synonymous with superior and
   consistent quality, whether or not a 'brand' in the conventional sense is used.

3. **Service.** Providing such a high level of service that customers will be
   naturally loyal and not want to switch to competitors.

4. **Building in 'cost to switch'.** Locking customers in, for example by pro-
   motional schemes such as Air Miles where customers are saving up for
   incentives and will not want to switch to another supplier, or by giving
   overriding discounts once a level of sales has been triggered, or even by
   supplying equipment (such as freezer cabinets for newsagents selling ice
   cream) that can be withdrawn if a competitor's product is bought, or in
   professional services by knowing so much about a client's business that it
   would take another supplier too long to 'come up to speed'.

5. **Locking up distribution channels.** Buying or having a special relationship with distributors that makes it difficult or impossible for a new supplier
   to get his product to the ultimate consumer: a policy followed for many
   years with great success, for example, in petrol retailing, where the superior
   siting of major oil companies' service stations helped them to sell their oil.

6. **Locking up sources of raw material supply.** Obtaining the best (or
   all) the product from its source either by owning the raw material (as with
   many large dairy companies) or by having a special relationship with suppliers, or by paying them more.

7. **Property/location.** Obtaining the best sites can be crucial in businesses as diverse as oil production and retailing. It is worth asking from time to time whether the desired location might change in the future and then moving to lock up suitable new sites, as for example in edge of town/out of town superstores.

8. **Expertise in hiring the best people.** Knowing how best to do something that is important to customers is an under-rated barrier The key is to locate the functional expertise that is most important and then make sure that your firm is better than any other at this. For example, in mass market retailing the buying and merchandising function is crucial. Wal-Mart, the leading US retailer, has a huge advantage because it has the best buyers and best relationships with suppliers. Hiring the best people can be a winning tactic, although only if the people can fit into the culture or the culture can be adapted to make best use of the newcomers.

9. **Proprietary expertise/patents.** The logical extension to 8 above in many businesses is a patent and in some businesses such as pharmaceuticals patents are hugely important in leading to much higher margins than would otherwise apply. Intellectual property can apply to a surprising range of businesses and it is worth checking whether anything your firm possesses can be patented.

10. **Lowest cost producer.** One of the very best barriers is to be able to produce a product or service for a particular market at a lower cost than competitors, usually by having larger scale in that SEGMENT than competitors and defending that relative advantage ferociously. To be most effective the cost advantage should be passed through in the form of lower prices, although spending more than competitors can match in terms of advertising, sales force or research can also be an effective way of using a cost (and margin) advantage to build barriers.

11. **Competitive response.** Making it clear to competitors that you will defend 'your patch', if necessary by 'crazy' actions, is a very effective barrier to entry. If a competitor ignores the warnings and enters, the response must be immediate and crushing, for example by dropping prices to its potential customers.

12. **Secrecy.** Sometimes a profitable market is relatively small and its existence or profitability may not be known by competitors. Keeping these segments well hidden from competitors can be very important, if necessary by obscuring or playing down their importance to your firm. Conversely, someone seeking to enter a market should invest properly in information about all potential customers.

BARRIERS TO EXIT

Exit barriers are undesirable forces that keep too many competitors in a market and lead to over-capacity and low profitability, because firms believe it is too expensive to leave the business. Barriers to exit may be real or imagined, economic or illusory, as the list below shows. In general, too much thought is given to barriers to exit and too little to barriers to entry.

1. **Redundancy costs.** The cost of paying off employees may be very heavy and much larger than the annual loss in a business. If a company is strapped for cash, it may find it easier to carry on in the short term and hope that others in the business will remove capacity first, thus postponing and perhaps removing the need to spend cash laying off the workforce. More of a problem in the US than most developing countries, more in the UK than the US, and more in most Continental countries than the UK, because of higher statutory pay-off provisions.

2. **Investment write-offs.** Quitting a business may cause a write-off of expensive plant and machinery that can only be used in that business. This leads to a feeling that the investment is being wasted and to a large one-time loss going through the profit and loss statement and a reduction of net assets in the balance sheet. This reason is, however, usually a very bad one for not quitting a loss-making business, since it refers to paper entries and not to industrial reality. A business which ought to have a write-off but does not is no more valuable, and probably less valuable, than a business that bites the bullet. The stock market understands this, and often large losses and write-offs from closing a business lead to an increase in share price, as investors are relieved by management's realism and look forward to the elimination of losses in the business.

3. **Real disengagement costs.** Leaving a business may sometimes lead to real, one-off costs other than labour ones. For example, a quarry may have to pay to restore the countryside to its previous glory, or a shop may have to carry out improvements before leaving. One of the most serious disengagement costs has been long leases on property that cannot be re-let at rates as high as the business is paying, and which would still need to be paid once the business has closed.

4. **Shared costs.** Often leaving one loss-making business is difficult because it would leave another profit-making business with higher costs, where these are shared between the two. For example, a factory may make two products and have shared overhead (and sometimes labour) costs, or a sales force may sell two products to the same customers. Very often, however, shared costs are an excuse for inaction. The proper answer, wherever possible (and how-

ever painful), is to slim down the overheads for the profitable business to what is necessary for that business after exiting the unprofitable one.

5. **Customers require a 'package'.** Customers sometimes value the provision of multiple products by the same supplier and would be reluctant or unwilling to buy from one that merely supplied the profitable products. For instance, a supermarket that refused to sell loss leaders such as baked beans or milk might find itself short of customers. Very often, however, this claim is a spurious excuse and customers would continue to buy a narrower product range provided this had a real advantage to them.

6. **Non-economic reasons.** Barriers to exit are very often openly non-economic, as when a government or trade union requires the business to be kept open and has the power to enforce this. More covert non-economic reasons include management ego or emotional attachment to a business, fear (normally unfounded or exaggerated) that it will affect a business's image and relationships in the trade, or simply opting for the line of least resistance. Non-economic reasons are increasingly becoming discredited, although they can work to your advantage when you are less sentimental than your competitors or when they face less economically numerate governments.

BCG BOSTON MATRIX

See GROWTH/SHARE MATRIX.

BUSINESS ATTRACTIVENESS

An assessment of how attractive a business or market is, based on a number of criteria. Often a distinction is made between the attractiveness of the market, on the one hand, based on factors such as market growth, average industry profitability, BARRIERS TO ENTRY (which should be high), BARRIERS TO EXIT (preferably low), the bargaining power of customers and suppliers (ideally low), the predictability of technological change, the protection against substitutes and, on the other hand, the strength of the individual company's business within the market, based on relative market share, brand strength, cost position, technological expertise and other such assessments. One can then produce a matrix and plot all a firm's businesses on the matrix to see where scarce corporate resources such as cash and good management should be allocated.

The matrix is an alternative to the BCG MATRIX and has the advantage that it can take into account several factors in evaluating the attractiveness of both business and market. On the other hand the lack of quantification of the axes can be a subjective trap, with management unwilling to admit that businesses are not attractive. Hence we use relative market share on the x axis, which in the long run is the most reliable indicator for business strength within a market. For any overall corporate plan it is useful to position all businesses on both matrices, and see whether the prescriptions are at all different. If they are, you should carefully examine the assumptions leading to the difference.

BUSINESS SEGMENT

A defensible competitive arena within which market leadership is valuable.

Contrast market segment, which is usually defined by market researchers' preordained categorization of the population into social class or psychologically defined groups, and much less useful. A business segment is an area within which a firm can specialize and gain competitive advantage. An example of a business segment would be high performance sports cars, which is a defensible market against mass market cars (at least for the time being). Thus Ferrari does not have to worry about its share of the overall car market if it can be the leader in its own segment. On the other hand, companies cannot define the market in a way that gives them market leadership and ipso facto call that a business segment. For example, red cars are not a separate segment from black cars, because specializing in red cars would not result in either extra consumer appeal or lower cost for producing red cars, and would therefore not be a defensible segmentation. See also SEGMENTATION for a much fuller discussion.

CASH COW

A business that is highly cash positive as a result of being a market leader in a means of very large low growth market. Such a business typically requires only moderate investment in physical assets or working capital, so that high profits result in high cash flow.

Cash cows are one of the four positions on the BCG MATRIX. In the BCG theory, cash from cash cows can be used to support other businesses that are leaders or potential leaders in high growth markets and that need cash to improve or maintain their market share position.

The BCG theory has often been misinterpreted, partly as a result of the tag 'cash cow'. Cows need to be milked, so the natural (but incorrect) inference is that the main role of cash cows is to give cash to the rest of the portfolio. Yet the original BCG theory stressed the point that cash cows should have the first call on their own cash: whatever investment was necessary to support the cash cows' position should come first. This common-sense prescription is often overlooked. Cash cows are not glamorous, and generally require only moderate amounts of grass, but they should still be allowed to graze on the most verdant pastures. It would have saved everyone a great deal of trouble if BCG had stuck to another name for cash cows, namely gold mines. Nobody would dream of denying a goldmine its required share of the budget.

COMB ANALYSIS

A very useful and simple technique for comparing customers' purchase criteria with their rating of suppliers. Let us assume that you are a textile manufacturer producing women's clothes and selling them to retailers who are fashion specialists. You want to find out what the most important reasons are for them to choose one manufacturer rather than another. You also want to find out what the retailers think about you and your competitors on each of these purchase criteria.

You should engage independent researchers to interview the retailers and ask them two questions. First, on a 1–5 scale, the importance of various purchase criteria. Let us assume that the average results are as shown in Illustration II.3. These results can now be displayed on the first part of the 'comb' chart (Illustration II.4).

The second question is how each of the competing suppliers rates on each of these criteria, again on a 1–5 scale. Let us start by overlaying on the previous results (the retailers' purchase criteria) their rating of the company sponsoring the research, which we will call Gertrude Textiles (Illustration II.5)

ILLUSTRATION II.3
Example of comb analysis

Criterion	Importance score
Fashion appeal of garments	4.9
Strength of brand name	4.6
Service and speed of delivery	4.5
Willingness to deliver small orders	3.5
Price from manufacturer to them	3.0
Durability of garments	2.3

ILLUSTRATION II.4

Comb chart retailers' purchase criteria

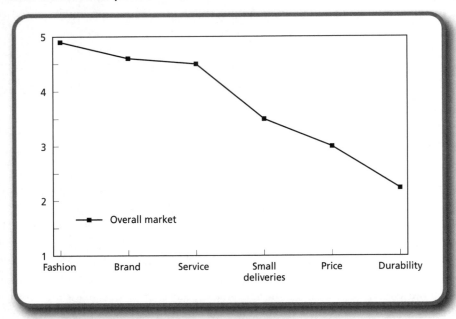

ILLUSTRATION II.5

Comb chart retailers' purchase criteria and their rating of Gertrude Textiles on these criteria

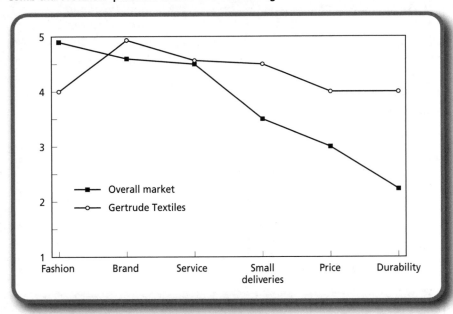

These results should be of great interest to Gertrude Textiles. Except on one criterion, Gertrude manages to score above the importance of the criteria to the retailer. Unfortunately, the one criterion on which Gertrude scores below market expectations is the most important one: the fashion appeal of its clothes. To increase market share, Gertrude Textiles must focus on improving its garments' fashion appeal. Of interest too is that on the last three criteria – willingness to deliver small quantities, price and the durability of its clothes – Gertrude scores above what the market requires. No doubt this is costing Gertrude a lot of money. This comb profile suggests that Gertrude could afford to not be so accommodating on small deliveries, could raise prices and could stop building in long life to its clothes. The money saved should be invested in doing whatever is necessary to improve perceptions of its fashion appeal – perhaps by luring the top designer team from a rival.

Then we come to the rating of competitors. We can now overlay on the previous picture the ratings given by retailers to two of Gertrude's rivals: Fast Fashions and Sandy's Styles (Illustration II.6). From this come three important observations:

ILLUSTRATION II.6

Comb chart: rating of three competitors against market criteria

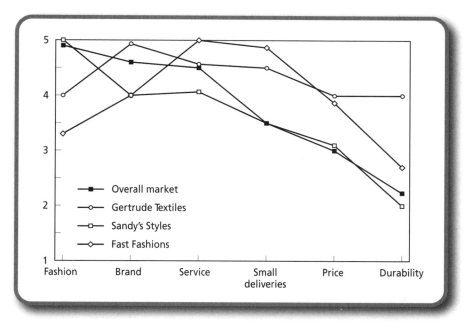

1. The only competitor that meets the market's very high fashion requirements is Sandy's Styles. This is the team for Gertrude Textiles to poach or beat.

2. Gertrude has the best brand name, according to the retailers and can meet all the purchase criteria apart from fashion. If this criterion can be met, Gertrude will be in a very strong position to increase market share.

3. Only Gertrude is significantly over-performing on the price requirements of retailers. This helps to confirm that Gertrude may be able to afford some price increases to retailers, particularly if the fashion element improves.

COMMODITY

With undifferentiated products, where suppliers are doomed to compete on price, branding has no value and the low-cost competitor will be able to earn higher returns and/or gain market share at the expense of his weaker (higher cost) brethren. Actually, commodity markets are often the result of a lack of imagination and marketing flair on the part of the participants. Almost anything can be successfully branded, and a price premium extracted. Take baked beans as an example: easy to produce and, you might think, a classic commodity market. Yet brilliant advertising based on brand identity – 'Beanz Meanz Heinz' – enabled Heinz to become market leader and extract a high price premium at the same time. Or another example where a commodity market was transformed into a branded market: flour. This is a large market where the competing products are almost indistinguishable in functional performance. So competition used to be based on fierce price discounting. Until, that is, RHM turned the other market upside down with its branded marketing campaign for Homepride based on the bowler-hatted flour-grader and the slogan: 'Graded grains make finer flour.' RHM gained both market share and a price premium.

Many industrial companies have discovered also that markets previously thought to be 'commodity' bear gardens can be turned into higher margin ones where one competitor gains an advantage based on service, technical excellence, industrial branding, or some other attribute of value to buyers.

COMPETENCY, COMPETENCIES

Skills that an organization has, what it is good at. Much recent thinking has stressed that an organization's operating skills relative to competition are at least as important to its success as its strategy is. To be successful an organization must be at least as good as its competition in certain key competencies. For example, in retailing, one of the most important skills is buying and merchandising, that is, procuring goods that consumers will want to buy and displaying them attractively. This very obvious statement explains in large part why some retailers, such as The Gap or Wal-Mart, are consistently more successful than their market rivals. Assessing and improving competencies (relative to competition) has rightly become the top priority for many managements.

CORE COMPETENCY

Similar to the idea of a corporation's 'distinctive competence' (the phrase coined by Phillip Selznick in 1955) or 'distinctive capabilities', the idea of core competencies was put forward by C.K. Prahalad and Gary Hamel in a renowned 1990 *Harvard Business Review* article. Prahalad and Hamel defined core competencies as:

> *'the collective learning in the organization, especially how to co-ordinate diverse production skills and integrate multiple streams of technology ... unlike physical assets, competencies do not deteriorate as they are applied and shared. They grow.'*

To be valuable, core competencies must add something really substantial to customers; they must be unique or at least rare; they must be difficult to imitate, and they must be able to be used effectively by the organization. The concept of core competencies became extremely fashionable in the 1990s, and it does have a great deal to commend it. Still, it is remarkably difficult for organizations to decide what their core competencies are, while at the same time avoiding wishful thinking. One problem is that if core competencies are defined in a sufficiently rigorous and precise way, they may prove not to be relevant to many businesses within the corporation. These businesses should be divested. But since managers tend to like to hang on to what they've got, they often fudge the issue and define the core competencies in too inclusive a way. The danger then is that the core competencies become meaningless; they do not realistically describe any competitive advantage.

Another problem is that core competency theory starts with the characteristics of the operating businesses rather than those of the parent organization (the center); the latter may be a better approach to corporate strategy.

Therefore it may be that, like BCG's growth/share matrix, the idea of core competencies is more valuable at the business unit level than at the corporate level, despite having been designed for the latter.

COSTS OF COMPLEXITY

A very important idea is that the more complex a business, the higher the costs, for any given level of scale. Complexity can mitigate the advantages of additional scale or even overturn them. Complexity arises when a firm extends its product line, customers, areas of expertise and/or use of different technologies in order to expand. The wise firm seeks extra scale without extra complexity, or reduces complexity without sacrificing scale.

Complexity cannot be avoided and is often market-driven. What separates the operationally skilful firm from others is very often its ability to manage customer-demanded complexity simply: providing customized or preferably customerized products with little added internal complexity.

But very often complexity is self-inflicted rather than market-driven. Customers may say they want a special product or service but be unwilling to pay for the real extra cost: they do not want it badly enough. And in many cases complexity has nothing to do with the customer but merely reflects bad management, and is often against the interests of both the firm and the customer. Production systems that resemble spaghetti, poor factory layouts, unnecessary stages in the production process, quality control departments (instead of building quality into the line), excess staff numbers and too many functional boundaries, insistence on doing everything within the firm rather than outsourcing wherever possible, interfering head office functions – all of these are complexity own-goals.

Waging war on complexity can lead simultaneously to stunning cost reductions and improvements in customer value. About half of all the value-added costs in the average firm are complexity-related, and half of these provide opportunities for radical cost reduction. Some tips for reducing the costs of complexity are reducing the number of suppliers and entering more collaborative relationships with them; buying in components and services wherever possible rather than 'making' them yourself; avoiding products or customers where added complexity is not fully compensated; eliminating complexity from product design and making product families modular; reducing the number of process steps; improving factory layout; creating small business units within the firm that take charge of a whole product/process from design to customer delivery; decimating head office; abolishing management hierarchy; reducing the information collected and disseminated; and generally not doing anything that is not essential to making customers happy. See AVERAGE COSTING AND PRICING and VALUE CHAIN.

DIVERSIFICATION

Being in or moving towards being a group of companies engaged in several different products and markets. Diversification is usually driven by the wish (or financial ability) to expand beyond the apparent limits of existing markets, and/or by the wish to reduce business risk by developing new 'legs'.

Many forests have been destroyed by writers praising and damning diversification. The balance of recent opinion has been against diversification (as in 'stick to the knitting'), although this has not stopped conglomerates (diversified companies) gaining a larger and larger share of corporate activity throughout the world, and especially in Britain.

The main justifications behind diversification are:

◆ **Financial.** *The* BCG MATRIX *developed a theory in the late 1960s that central management of successful firms can and should shovel cash around the corporation in order to move it away from businesses that would always consume cash and into those few businesses that have the potential for market leadership and long-term cash generation. This was a rather selective theory of diversification, but Bruce Henderson became an apostle of conglomerates, convinced that the strategically directed conglomerate could continually compound its cash generation capability and expand the scope of its operations. Modern financial theorists counter that shareholders, not managers, should diversify their holdings and that it is better for shareholders to be offered a selection of 'pure plays' of non-diversified companies.*

◆ **Management skills.** *Several diversified companies such as Hanson and BTR are highly skilled at identifying under-performing companies and at changing management structures and behavior in order to improve performance. Diversification of this type involves buying, fixing, and at the right time selling, such companies.*

◆ **Core skills or** COMPETENCIES. *A company's expertise may not really reside in knowing a particular market, but in certain skills that are applicable across several markets.*

Companies must not fool themselves about whether they have competencies that are applicable in new areas. But a moment's thought is usually all that is necessary to dismiss many instances of clear wishful thinking. The most notorious instances of unsuccessful diversification could not have been justified by the principle of core skills. Had this principle been the touchstone, Cummins, the world leader in diesel engines, would not have gone into ski resort development; Letraset, the world specialist in dry transfers, would not have bought stamp dealer Stanley Gibbons; General Mills would not have ventured from food manufacturing into toys; Coca-Cola would not have gone into the film industry by buying Columbia Pictures; and Lex Service, the car dealer and importer, would not have gone into the specialist world of electronic distribution.

All good diversification builds on competitive advantage in core businesses and reinforces rather than detracts from that by strengthening the competencies that drive success in the existing businesses. This is true even though the product areas may seem only tangentially related, as in Marks and Spencer's inspired move from clothes retailing to selling a narrow line of up-market foods. The core competencies of buying and merchandising, branding, stock management and customer care were reinforced by the diversification, even though at the time it seemed to many observers an odd move. See also ANSOFF MATRIX.

DOG

1. Bad business, candidate for disposal.

2. Term invented by BCG to describe a company's low relative market share businesses (i.e. those that are not market leaders) in low-growth markets (those growing at less than 10 per cent a year). BCG originally said that dogs (which it called 'pets' in the early days) were unlikely to be very cash positive or to be capable of being driven to market leadership; dogs should therefore be sold or closed. Since a majority of nearly all firms' businesses are dogs, this advice is draconian indeed, and was later soft-pedaled by BCG. Dogs are in fact often quite cash positive, especially if they are STRONG FOLLOWERS (i.e. not very much smaller than the market leader). It is also untrue that dogs cannot be driven to market leadership (i.e. become CASH COWS), though this is less usual than for followers in high growth markets (QUESTION MARKS). See GROWTH/SHARE MATRIX and MARKET CHALLENGER.

EIGHTY/TWENTY RULE, 80/20 RULE, 80/20 PRINCIPLE

The Pareto rule, that 80 per cent of sales come from 20 per cent of the products. Can clearly be looked at empirically in any case, and usually one of the most valuable simplest steps to understanding any business. Invented by Vilfredo Pareto, the nineteenth-century economist. Looked at in retrospect, many of the insights in the past half century are derived from the Pareto principle, including BCG's focus on those few high relative market share businesses that generate most of the cash for a company; the insight that COSTS OF COMPLEXITY derive from too extensive a product range; that maximum use should be made of out-sourcing; the movement to rationalize stock-holding; and conducting ABC analysis of true profitability.

The 80/20 rule applies to individuals as well: 80 per cent of the value you provide in your job may come from 20 per cent of your time, so if you dele-gated the activities that take the remaining 80 per cent of your time to a lower cost or less experienced person (or stopped doing them altogether) you could multiply your effect up to five times. For both firms and individuals, some of the low-value 80 per cent may actually have negative value. Perhaps firms should legislate that all of their people spend at least 15 minutes a week con-templating the 80/20 rule. (Or that they should all buy Richard Koch's bestseller *The 80/20 Principle!*)

EXPERIENCE CURVE

Along with the BCG matrix, the greatest discovery of Bruce Henderson, although it started life in 1926 as the 'learning curve'. Briefly, it states that when the accumulated production of any good or service doubles, unit costs in real terms (i.e. adjusted for inflation) have the potential to fall by 20-30 per cent. Accumulated production is not a concept much used, nor is it usually very easy to calculate: it is the total number of units of a product that have ever been made by a firm, or the total number of units of product ever made by all participants in the market. It is not related to time, because accumulated pro-duction can double within one year for new or very fast growth product, or take centuries for a very old or slow growth one.

BCG found and documented many exciting examples in the late 1960s and 1970s where accumulated production had increased rapidly and deflated (inflation-adjusted) costs had fallen to 70-80 per cent of their previous level each time this happened. One of the most important examples is the decline in the cost of integrated circuits (ICs), which explains why the cost of com-puters was able to plummet so dramatically. A typical example of a cost experience curve is shown in Illustration II.7.

GROWTH/GROWTH MATRIX

Useful two-by-two chart invented by BCG. Compares the growth of a firm's business in one product or BUSINESS SEGMENT to the growth of the market as a whole, enabling one to see whether market share was being won or lost and by whom.

ILLUSTRATION II.7
Cost experience curve

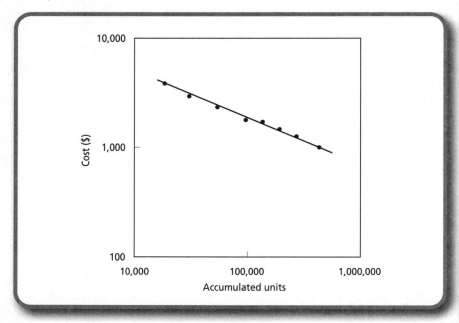

Source: Automobile Manufacturer's Association. BCG Analysis

Illustration II.8 shows an example, using imaginary data, of three competitors in a particular market at a particular time (three, five or ten years are generally used). According to the (made-up) data, the largest competitor is McKinsey, which is growing more slowly than the market as a whole (and therefore losing share); the next largest is BCG, which is growing at the same rate as the market; and the smallest but fastest growing competitor is Bain. Note that companies on a growth/growth chart are always at the same vertical height, since this represents the overall market growth and must by definition be common for all.

Growth/growth charts are not much used nowadays but are very useful, especially if used in conjunction with the main BCG matrix (the GROWTH/SHARE).

GROWTH/SHARE MATRIX

The Boston Consulting Group has invented several matrices, having trained its consultants to think in terms of two-by-two displays, but this is the most famous and useful one (it is also sometimes called the Boston or BCG MATRIX).

ILLUSTRATION II.8

Examples of growth/growth matrix with competitors arrayed

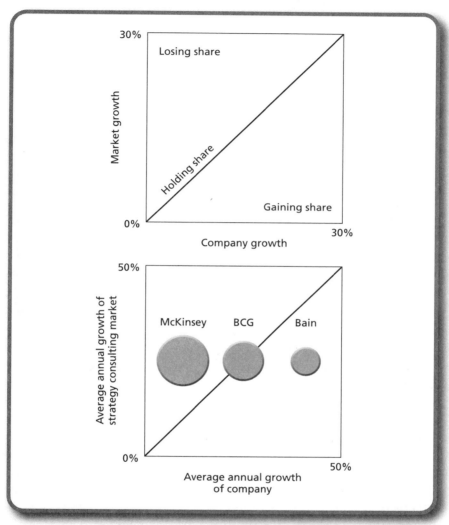

Invented in the late 1960s and still of great importance, it measures market growth and relative market share for all the business a particular firm has. An example is shown in Illustration II.9.

It is important to define the axes properly. The horizontal axis is of fundamental importance and measures the market share that a firm has in a particular business *relative to the share enjoyed in that business by its largest*

ILLUSTRATION II.9

Growth/share matrix for Engulf & Devour

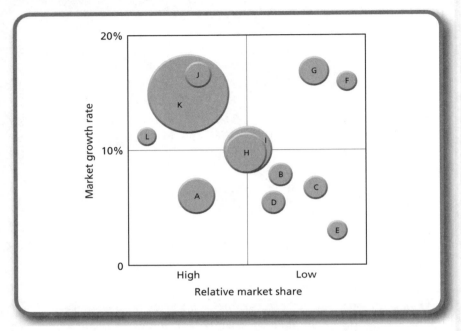

competitor. Thus if Engulf & Devour has a 40 per cent market share in Business A and its nearest competitor has a 10 per cent market share, its relative market share ('RMS') is 400 per cent or 4 times (written as 4.0x). In Business B, Engulf & Devour may have a 5 per cent share and the leading competitor 10 per cent, in which case Engulf & Devour's relative market share is 50 per cent or 0.5x. Note that absolute market share (for example, 20 per cent of a market) means little, because it could mean a relative market share of 0.33x (if the dominant competitor has 60 per cent market share), or of 10.0x (if the rest of the market is very fragmented and the next largest player has only 2 per cent).

The vertical axis is the growth rate of the market in which the business competes. Much confusion surrounds the precise definition of this market growth rate. The correct definition is the expected future annual growth rate (over the next five years) in volume (units of production) of the market as a whole, not of the particular Engulf & Devour business.

Before going on, it is important to understand the reasons why BCG and we think that the axes are significant. The relative market share is key because a business that is larger than its competitors (has a high relative market share, more than 1.0) ought to have lower costs, or higher prices, or both, and therefore higher profitability than a competitor in that business with a lower share. This is generally although not always, true, as confirmed by databases such as the PIMS studies.

It is also logical: a business with higher volume ought to be able to spread its fixed costs over more units, and therefore have lower fixed and overhead costs, as well as make better use of any expensive machinery or people that are the best for that particular business. The higher share business may also be able to charge a higher price, either because it has the best brand or because it has the best distribution or simply because it is the preferred choice of most people. Since price minus cost equals profit, the higher share competitor should have the highest margins, or be ploughing back his advantage in the form of extra customer benefits that will reinforce his market share advantage.

Note that we say that the higher share competitor ought to have lower costs or higher prices. It does not necessarily follow, since he may squander his potential advantage by inefficiency, sharing costs with unprofitable products, or by having poorer customer service than a rival. Where the higher share player does not have profits higher than competitors there is usually an unstable competitive relationship, which can create both opportunity and vulnerability in that market (see the OPPORTUNITY/VULNERABILITY MATRIX).

In some cases having a higher share of a market does not confer any benefit or potential benefit, for example where a one-man plumbing business faces a ten-man plumbing business, and the costs of labour are the same for everyone. Many people have claimed that the importance of market share, and the value of the growth/share matrix, have been greatly overstated, and produce examples of cases where larger businesses are less profitable than smaller businesses, or where there is no systematic difference in profitability according to scale. On detailed examination, however, there are few individual business segments where it is not or cannot be a real advantage to be larger, all other things being equal. The qualification in the last phrase is crucial: relative market share is not the only influence on profitability, and it may be overwhelmed by different competitors' operating skills or strategies, or random influences on profitability.

One cause of confusion is that businesses are often not defined properly, in a sufficiently disaggregated way, before measuring market share. The niche player who focuses on a limited product range or customer base may be playing in just one segment. The broad line supplier will be present in several segments and may actually not be very large in any one segment despite appearing to have a high overall market share. For example, a national supermarket chain may be bigger than competitors which have regional chains, but the relevant basis of competition may be local scale and customer awareness.

See BUSINESS SEGMENT and SEGMENTATION for the importance of correct business definition and some hints on how to do it.

If businesses are defined properly, the higher share competitor should have an advantage at least nine times out of ten. It therefore follows that the further to the left a business is on the BCG MATRIX, the stronger it should be.

What about the vertical axis: the growth rate of the market? BCG claimed that there was a real difference between high growth businesses (where demand is growing at 10 per cent or more) and lower growth ones, because of greater fluidity in the former: that is, if the market is growing fast, there is more opportunity to gain market share. This is logical, both because more new business is up for grabs, and because competitors will react much more vigorously to defend their absolute share (to avoid a loss of turnover) than to defend loss of relative share, which they do not even notice in a fast changing market.

Having understood these points, we can go on to characterize the four quadrants of the BCG matrix (see Illustration II.10).

The bottom left hand box contains the CASH COWS (called 'gold mines' in some early versions of the matrix: in many ways a better name). These busi-

ILLUSTRATION II.10
The quadrants of BCG's growth/share matrix

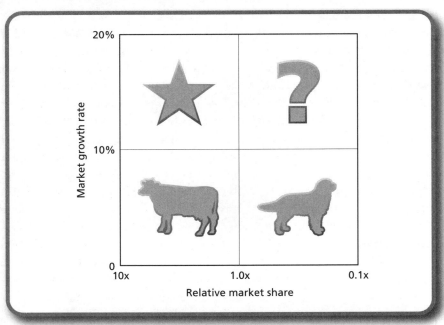

nesses have high relative market share (they are by definition market leaders) and therefore ought to be profitable. They are very valuable and should be protected at all costs. They throw off a lot of cash, which can be reinvested in the business, used elsewhere in the business portfolio, used to buy other businesses, or paid out to shareholders.

The top left box comprises STARS: high relative market share businesses in high growth markets. These are very profitable but may need a lot of cash to maintain their position. This cash should be made available. Whatever it takes to hold or gain share in star businesses should be undertaken. If they hold RMS, star businesses will become cash cows when the market growth slows down, and will therefore be hugely valuable over a long time. But if star businesses lose relative market share, as they are often allowed to do, they will end up as DOGS and be of limited value.

The top right box holds QUESTION MARKS (sometimes called wildcats): low RMS positions but in high growth markets. In this case 'question mark' is a very good description of the business, since it has an uncertain future, and the decision on whether to invest in the business is both important and difficult. If a question mark does not improve its relative market share − that is, if it remains a follower − it will end life as a DOG. On the other hand, if the volatility that market growth bestows is used and investment is made in a question mark to drive it into a leadership position, the business will migrate to being a star (profitable) and ends its days as a cash cow (very profitable and very cash-positive). The problem is that question mark businesses very often turn into cash traps, as money can be invested without any guarantee (and in some cases much chance) of attaining a leadership position. A business that is invested in heavily without attaining market leadership (like much of the British computer industry up to the 1980s) will simply be an investment in failure and a gross waste of money.

The bottom right box is the DOG kennel. Dogs are low relative market share positions in low growth businesses. The theory therefore says that they should not be very profitable and should not be able to gain share to migrate into cash cows. Given that the majority of most firm's businesses may be in this box, this is not a very cheerful notion.

In fact, the greatest weakness in the BCG theory relates to dogs, largely because of this fatalism. The later strategic view of DOGS puts the case for their defense and stresses ways in which dogs can often be made valuable parts of a firm's business portfolio. Briefly, dogs can migrate into cash cows, by resegmenting the business or simply by having greater customer responsiveness than the market leader. Even if leadership is not possible, it is usually worthwhile to improve market share position within the dog category. A business with a relative market share of 0.7x (70 per cent of the leader) may be quite profitable, highly cash positive and quite different from a business with an RMS of only 0.3x (30 per cent of the leader).

Nevertheless, it may be true that there is limited room for manoeuvre with dog businesses and they will generally be less attractive than stars or cash cows.

BCG superimposed on the growth/share matrix results a theory of cash management (sometimes confusingly called portfolio management), which is intriguing and makes some useful points, although it is also flawed. The theory looks at the cash characteristics of each of the quadrants (Illustration II.11). BCG's theory then came up with a hierarchy of uses of cash, numbered from 1 to 4 in order of priority (Illustration II.12).

1. The best use of cash is to defend cash cows. They should not need to use cash very often, but if investment in a new factory or technology is required, it should be made unstintingly.

2. The next call on cash should be in stars. These will need a great deal of investment to hold (or gain) relative market share.

ILLUSTRATION II.11

The growth/share matrix cash characteristics

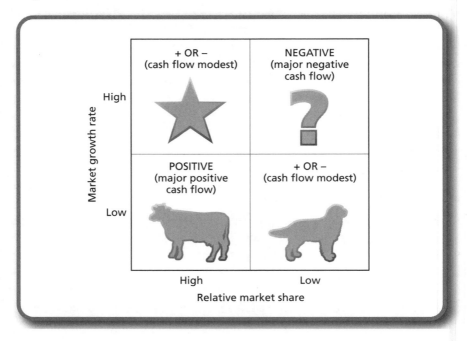

ILLUSTRATION II.12

How to use the cash

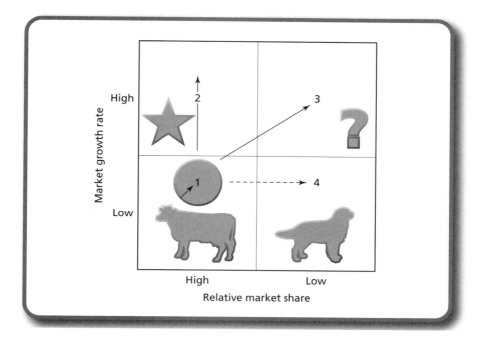

3. The trouble begins here, with BCG's third priority, to take money from cash cows and invest in question marks. The bastardized version of the theory stressed this cash flow in particular. BCG countered by stressing that investment in question marks should be selective, confined to those cases where there was a real chance of attaining market leadership. With this qualification, BCG's point is sensible.

4. The lowest priority was investment in dogs, which BCG said should be minimal or even negative, if they were run for cash. This may be a sensible prescription, but the problem is that the dog kennel may contain a large range of breeds with different qualities, and a differentiated cash strategy is generally required within the dog kennel.

A weakness of the BCG cash management theory, however, as BCG came to realize, was the assumption that the portfolio had to be in balance in respect of cash on an annual or three-year basis. In fact, the cash invested in the overall business portfolio does not have to equal the cash generated. Surplus cash can be invested outside of the existing portfolio, either by acquiring new businesses, by entering them from scratch, or by reducing debt or giving cash back to the shareholders. Conversely, if a business needs to invest more cash (for example, in an important and cash-guzzling star) than the business portfolio is generating, it should go out and raise the cash from bankers and/or shareholders to fund the cash gap. The business portfolio should not be thought of as a closed system.

The second weakness of BCG's views on cash, and one not fully realized until much later, was the implicit assumption that all businesses should be managed from the center in a cashbox-plus-strategic-control way. BCG's theory was immensely attractive to chairmen and chief executives seeking a sensible role for the center, and probably did a great deal more good than harm, but only a minority of businesses are run in this way. Indeed, the recent work by Goold, Campbell and Alexander largely divides businesses into just two categories: those that are run by financial control on the one hand and those that follow either strategic control or strategic planning on the other. These are two very different approaches, the former decentralized, the latter more centralized, and it is difficult to combine the two styles, as BCG's approach assumed. Perhaps, in the future, someone will devise a method of control that incorporates the strong points of both styles, but it will take much more than a two-by-two matrix to realize this vision.

The BCG MATRIX marked a major contribution to management thinking. From the mid to late 1970s BCG tended to retreat too much under the weight of critical comment, and the matrix is not much used today. It is overdue for a revival. Anyone who tries to apply it thoughtfully to his or her business will learn a lot during the process.

HARVESTING

Deliberate or unintentional running down of a business and its market share position in order to extract short term profit: 'selling' market share. Harvesting can result from a number of policies: holding or raising prices higher than competitors, not reinvesting in marketing and selling effort or in new equipment, or by stopping advertising. Such steps could result in a short-term increase in profits but the competitive position of the business will be weakened and with loss of market share it will end up as a smaller business, which may not even be viable in the medium term. Harvesting may happen without management being aware of it — reinvestment does not occur because it 'cannot be agreed', and market share is gradually lost — or if they do realize, without them connecting it to the failure to invest as much as competitors.

Harvesting as a deliberate strategy is not much practised, and for good reason: you cannot tell how fast market share will be lost, and the business can disappear into an irreversible doom loop much faster than expected. Harvesting can be a rewarding tactic, however, if it is intended to sell a business within a year or so. The final year's profits can be significantly boosted, and the buyer may apply a normal PE ratio to buy the business without realizing that it is losing market share and that the profits are not sustainable.

Harvesting, like so many other concepts, was the invention of the Boston Consulting Group. See BCG MATRIX.

INCREMENTAL SALES

Sales at a price that does not cover the fully incurred cost of a product or service, but which managers justify on the grounds that they cover some company overhead, or at least some manufacturing overhead.

Incremental sales are prevalent in industries with high fixed costs, such as the chemical, car and airline industries. When faced with assets that are not being useful, companies will prefer to keep their assets running and sell at a price that at least covers their raw material costs, and some overheads, instead of not making any money at all. For example, empty airline seats, where it may be better to charge a very low price at the last minute rather than leave unfilled.

Although the case for incremental sales is seductive, they can be damaging and need to be considered carefully. They drive down price. They can only be sold at unrealistically low prices because other products cover part of their real costs. Pretty soon competitors will have to follow suit, and often these products become structurally unprofitable.

Also, they make future investments in a business more difficult. While the incremental sales do not cover their costs, they do actually use production capacity and require attention. When you run into capacity constraints or shortage of staff, you could cut back on your incremental sales and thus alleviate the bottleneck. But you will probably have forgotten that you have a considerable volume of incremental sales, and instead increase capacity or staffing. Result – you invest and are bound to lower your rate of return.

The only way to avoid this trap is to be sure that you always compare making an investment or increasing staff with cutting out the lowest contributing product.

MARKET CHALLENGERS

STRONG FOLLOWER in market share terms: companies that are not far behind the market leader in a particular product or service. The term is not wholly satisfactory because it implies that the second or third player is gaining relative market share on the leader and challenging him. The term strong follower does not carry this implication, and is reserved for a RELATIVE MARKET SHARE of at least 0.7x, that is, at least 70 per cent the size of the leader. Neither term is widely used, hence the neglect of DOGS that may have potential. See DOGS.

MISSION

What a company is for; why it exists; its role in the world. This is an enormously important issue. Many companies have formal mission statements, but a big distinction must be made between such documents and the company having a real mission, or 'sense of mission'. Most companies that have mission statements do not have a sense of mission: the document is propaganda, or at best, well intended 'motherhood', but not what most people in the organization believe. Yet some firms such as Marks and Spencer that clearly have a sense of mission do not have mission statements.

A sense of mission is essential if employees are to believe in their company. They have to think that the company is there to achieve something. Why does it matter that employees believe in their company? Well, most would rather work for a company they can believe in. Such a company will attract the best recruits, and keep them. It will get the most out of its people, both as individuals and in teams. It will be respected by customers and investors. It will learn, renew itself and become more powerful, while still having the ethic of service to others. It will gain market share, and have the best long-term profitability, and the highest market rating.

All in all, a mission is important. Unfortunately, though most Western firms have mission statements, few have a sense of mission. Although precise data is not available, the best estimates are that 10 per cent of large UK firms, 20 per cent of those in the US, but 50 per cent of Japanese firms have a sense of mission. Clearly there is a need for transformation.

OPPORTUNITY/VULNERABILITY MATRIX

An interesting outgrowth from the BCG MATRIX, although not developed until the late 1970s/early 1980s (mainly by Bain & Company) and refined later that decade by the LEK Partnership, another strategy boutique. BCG had posited that high relative market share businesses (leaders) should be extremely profitable, and the logic of the EXPERIENCE CURVE certainly suggested that the higher the market share, the higher the profitability (unless the firm was not using its potential advantages or pricing to penetrate the market still further). It followed that it should be possible to construct a 'normative curve' to describe the profitability of the average BUSINESS SEGMENT in a particular industry, or, with a wider band, all industries, according to a normal expectation given the segment's relative market share. This normative band is shown on the matrix in Illustration II.13.

The area between the two curved lines represents the normative band: depending on the data used, perhaps 80 per cent of observations would fall between these broad limits, and it would be unusual (only 20 per cent of business segment positions) for businesses to fall outside the band. (The normative band can be constructed based on actual data of business segment positions and profitability, but only after correct segmentation: in practice such data can be obtained with any degree of confidence only after working within a client organization, and building up an anonymous database of the relationships. In fact, empirical data did enable the normative band to be built up in this way. The band used to be shaded in yellow, hence the chart became known as a 'bananagram'.)

So what? Well, one implication is that high relative market share positions, correctly segmented, are as valuable as BCG said, whatever reservations one has about the EXPERIENCE CURVE. Managers should therefore strive to be in such businesses and cannot expect to have profitability above the required rate of return of investors unless a majority of their sales are in leaders or strong followers (at least 0.7x relative market share, that is, at least 70 per cent of the leader in the segment).

Another implication, not really made clearly by BCG, and in some ways obscured by the doctrine of the BCG matrix about DOGS, was that it was useful to improve relative market share in a business segment whatever the starting position: useful to take a 0.3x RMS business and move it to a 0.6x RMS position, to take a 0.5x position and take it to 1.0x, to take a 2x position and move it to 4x, and so on. Illustration II.13 enables one to calculate roughly what equilibrium profitability can be expected from any particular position, so that it is possible to state roughly the benefit of moving any particular segment position in this way and compare with to the expected short term cost of doing so (by extra marketing or service, product development or lower prices). In this way it can be seen (a) whether it is worth trying to raise RMS and (b) which segments give the biggest bang for the buck.

ILLUSTRATION II.13
Opportunity/vulnerability matrix

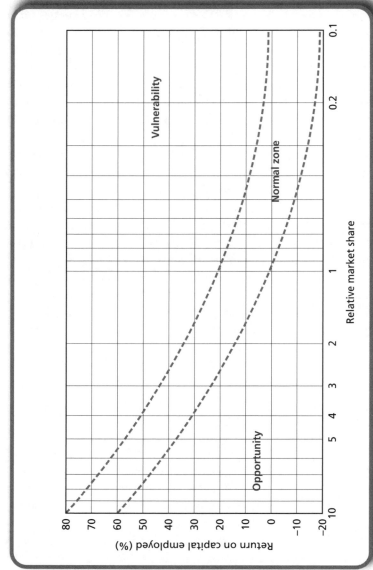

But the most valuable use of the matrix lies not in the 80 per cent of positions that fall within the banana (normative curve), but rather in the 20 per cent that fall outside. Two examples of possible such positions are given in that business Illustration II.14. Business A is earning (say) 45 per cent return on capital employed, a good return, but is in a weak relative market share position (say 0.5x, or only half share position the size of the segment leader). The theory and empirical data from the matrix suggest that the combination of these two positions is at best anomalous, and probably unsustainable. Business A is therefore in the 'vulnerability' part of the matrix. The expectation must be that in the medium-term, either the business must improve its relative market share position to sustain its profitability (the dotted arrow moving left), or that it will decline in profitability (to about breakeven). Why should this happen? Well, the banana indicates that the market leader in this business may well be earning 40 per cent or even more ROCE in the segment (the beauty of the method is that this can be investigated empirically). What may be happening is that the leader is holding a price umbrella over the market: that is, is pricing unsustainably high, so that even the competitors with weak market share are protected from normal competitive rainfall. What happens if the market leader suddenly cuts prices by 20 per cent?

ILLUSTRATION II.14

Opportunity/vulnerability matrix showing positions of business outside the banana

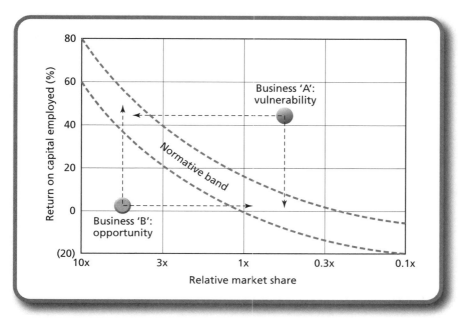

He will still earn a good return, but the weaker competitors will not. (The leader may not cut prices, but instead provide extra product benefits or service or other features, but the effect would still be a margin cut.) It is as well to know that business A is vulnerable. If relative market share cannot be improved, it is sensible to sell it before the profitability declines.

Now let's look at business B. This is a business in a strong relative market share position. The leader in this segment is earning 2 per cent ROCE. This is a wonderful business to find. The theory and practical data suggest that such a business should be making 50 per cent ROCE, not 2 per cent. Nine times out of ten when such businesses are found it is possible to make them very much more profitable, usually by radical cost reduction, but sometimes through radical improvement of the service and product offering to the customer at low extra cost to the supplier, but enabling a large price hike to be made. Managements of particular businesses very often become complacent with historical returns and think it is impossible to raise profits in a step function to three, four or five times their current level. The bananagram challenges that thinking for leadership segment positions and usually the bananagram is proved right. After all, high relative market share implies huge potential advantages; but these must be earned and exploited, as they do not automatically disgorge huge profits.

PARENT, PARENTING ADVANTAGE

The useful concept invented by the Ashridge Strategic Management Center, which is to corporate strategy what 'competitive advantage' is to business unit strategy. Parenting advantage exists when the parent or center is the best possible owner of a business, because it adds more value to the business than any other potential parent. Unless there is parenting advantage for any business under the parent's control, the business should be divested.

PORTER'S FIVE COMPETITIVE FORCES

Michael Porter was an innovator in structural analysis of markets, which previously, even with BCG, tended to focus largely on direct competition in the industry, without looking systematically at the context in other stages of the industry VALUE CHAIN. Porter's five forces to analyse are:

1. Threat from potential new entrants.
2. Threat from substitutes using different technology.
3. Bargaining power of customers.
4. Bargaining power of suppliers.
5. Competition among existing suppliers.

The interactions between the five forces are shown in Illustration II.15. From this Porter builds a useful model of industry attractiveness and how this might change over time, both because of objective economic changes and also because of the ambitions of the players themselves.

ILLUSTRATION II.15
Porter's five competitive forces

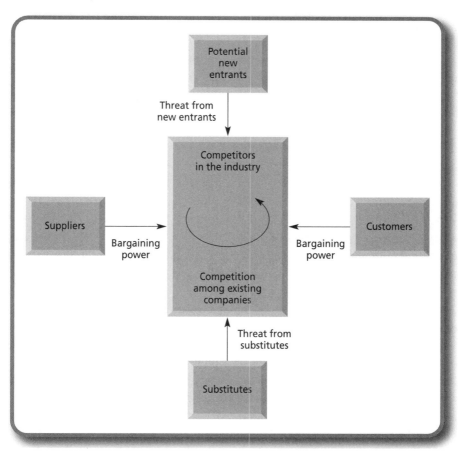

QUESTION MARK

A firm's position in a business segment where the market is growing fast (expected future volume growth of 10 per cent or more per annum) but the firm is a follower, that is, has a RELATIVE MARKET SHARE of less than 1.0x. One of the four positions on the BCG MATRIX. Unlike two of the others, very well named: there is a real question about such businesses that must be faced. Should the corporation invest a lot of cash and management talent to try to drive that business to a leading position, hence becoming a STAR (high market growth, high relative market share) and eventually a much bigger and highly positive CASH COW? Or should the business be sold for a high price earnings ratio, because people pay highly for 'growth' businesses without usually thinking too hard about the relative market share position? There is another option, which is usually taken, and usually wrong: putting some cash into the business but not enough to drive it to a leading position. The BCG theory and observation both lead to the conclusion that this will tend to give a poor return on the cash invested: the business will eventually become a DOG, and though it may throw off rather more cash in this state than the original BCG theory, it is unlikely to show a very good return on the cash invested.

So, is it to be investment to drive to leadership, or a quick and lucrative sale? It depends, of course, on the sums involved, but particularly on whether you think leadership is attainable at acceptable cost. And then it depends on the reaction of the current leader, who has the STAR position: he ought to defend it to the death, but may not. Getting into this kind of battle is unpredictable and like playing poker: once started, you have to keep upping the ante to persuade the opponent that you will win in the end; and if you are to cut your losses at any stage, you had better do it early. What is the size of your pot of cash compared with his? The strength of your hand versus his is also very important. Do you have the knack of satisfying customers better, or higher quality, or better people or better technology, or just greater will power and commitment, or preferably all of the above?

STAR positions are enormously valuable once obtained and defended. But most attempts to back question marks fail to turn them into stars. Unless you are determined to win and have a greater-than-even chance, sale is usually the option that will better enhance shareholder wealth. As a shareholder you should hope that the latter consideration weighs more heavily with the management than wanting to stay in a glamorous growth business.

RELATIVE MARKET SHARE (RMS)

The share of a firm in a BUSINESS SEGMENT divided by the share of the firm's largest competitor. Much more important than market share as an absolute number. For example, if Sony's nearest competitor in making Discman-type products is one tenth the size, Sony will have an RMS of 10 times (written as 10x, or 10.0x, or sometimes simply 10). The competitor, on the other hand, will have an RMS that is the reciprocal of this: it will have an RMS of 0.1x.

One more example will suffice: if Coca-Cola in one national market has a market share of 60 per cent, and Pepsi-Cola 30 per cent, then Coke has an RMS of 2x, and Pepsi 0.5x.

Relative market share should correlate with profitability. If it does not, one (or more) of five things is happening:

1. The business segment has been defined incorrectly.

2. The smaller competitor is much cleverer than the bigger. The leader is not using his potential advantage properly, and/or the follower has found a nifty way to lower costs or raise prices that has overcome the leader's advantages of scale and experience.

3. The leader is forfeiting profit by expensive reinvestment that will compound his advantage in the future and lead to much higher profits.

4. There is over-capacity in the industry so the main concern is capacity utilization, and the bigger competitors may simply have too much of the excess.

5. It is a business not susceptible to normal scale, status and experience effects.

Let us take each of these in turn. (1) Incorrect business definition: more often than not, this is the reason. In most cases, the segment will not have been defined in a sufficiently disaggregated way. (2) A clever follower. This does happen, and is usually manifest in a refusal to play by the usual rules of the game. (3) Long-term compounding strategy by the leader. May be true if it is Japanese or Korean, almost certainly not otherwise. (4) Excess capacity: yes, sometimes. (5) Industry and business not susceptible to scale, experience or status: very rare. Even service businesses generally are skewed in favor of the bigger players, who have greater advantages in terms of branding, reputation, lower marketing and selling costs, and greater expertise and ability to attract the best recruits.

One of the most useful charts to draw for any business, if the data can be collected, is shown in Illustration II.16, which looks at the profitability (in terms of ROS or ROCE) of different competitors in a business segment. It shows a typical pattern, but the beauty of the method is that empirical data

ILLUSTRATION II.16

Typical pattern of profitability by RMS

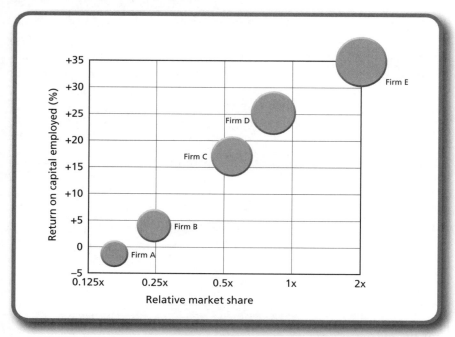

can be displayed to see whether and how far the expected pattern applies. If there is deviance from the normal pattern, the reasons given in (1) to (5) above can be systematically investigated.

The chart stops at 2x (two times) RMS only because in this case the leader was here. In other examples the relationship has been observed to continue working over whatever range of RMS applies. Businesses with a 10x RMS really do make very high ROCE – normally in the 60–90 per cent range.

Observation of this relationship led to the development of a very useful tool – the OPPORTUNITY/VULNERABLE MATRIX. See this entry for the action implications of RMS and profit relationships.

SEGMENTATION

Most usefully, the process of analyzing customers, costs and competitors in order to decide where and how to wage the competitive battle; or a description of the competitive map according to the contours of the business segments. Sadly, segmentation is often used to describe a more limited (and often misleading) exercise in dividing up customer groups. See BUSINESS SEG-MENT. Proper segmentation takes place only at the level of identifying the BUSINESS SEGMENT: this is at the root of any firm's business strategy. Segmentation in this most useful sense is what is discussed below.

It is crucial for any firm to know which segments it is operating in, to know its relative market share in those segments, and to focus on those segments where it has or can build a leadership position. A segment is a competitive system, or arena, where it is possible to build barriers against other firms, by having lower costs or customer-satisfying differentiation (which will be expressed in higher prices, and/or in higher customer volume which itself will lead to lower costs). A segment can be a particular product, or a particular customer group being sold a standard product, or a particular customer group being sold a special product or provided with a special service, or a particular distribution channel or region, or any combination of the above. What matters is that the following conditions for a genuine segment are all satisfied:

1. The segment must be capable of clear distinction, so that there is no doubt which customers and products fall inside and outside the segment.

2. The segment must have a clear and limited set of competitors that serve it.

3. It must be possible to organize supply of a product or service to the segment in a way that represents some specialization, and is differentiated from supply to another or other segments.

4. The segment must have purchase criteria that are different in important ways from other segments.

5. The segment must be one where competitors specialize, and where there is a characteristic market share ranking that can be described.

6. The segment must be capable of giving at least one competitor a profitability advantage, either by having lower costs, or higher prices, than other competitors, or both.

7. It must be possible to build barriers around the segment to deter entrants.

Segmentation may change over time. To take the example of the motor car, Henry Ford created his own segment around the black Model T Ford: the mass produced, standard automobile. Initially, he had 100 per cent of this segment, and it satisfied all of the rules above. Later, he provided other colors at relatively low cost, and General Motors changed the mass automobile market to include any color, standard car: the 'black car' segment ceased to exist and became part of a wider competitive arena. Subsequently new segments emerged, based on sports/high performance criteria, and later on 'compact' low fuel consumption cars.

Geography is a fascinating and changing dimension of segmentation. Most products and services start out by having a very limited geographical reach: one region or one country. The UK potato crisp (US potato chips) market is an interesting example. At one time the market was dominated by Smiths, then by Golden Wonder (which led the way in introducing a range of flavor), both national competitors. Then, gradually, a regional competitor, Walkers, emerged, based on superior quality. Initially, Walkers' segment boundaries were restricted to the Midlands where the company was based. Within this region the national segmentation did not rule: Walkers was the top supplier by a long way, although nationally very small. Gradually, with greater production and improved distribution, Walkers became a national competitor, and for a time market leader, again causing the segmentation to revert to a national level.

An increasing number of markets are global: the battle between Pepsi and Coke, for instance, is fought beyond the boundaries of individual countries. Nevertheless, segment RELATIVE MARKET SHARE positions often vary significantly in different countries: if Pepsi outsells Coke in one national market, against the global trend, that national market is today a separate segment. If, on the other hand, relative market shares around the world converge, the whole world can become one segment for cola drinks. Economics comes into this as well. To take one far-fetched example, assume that Coke came to have a two to one advantage over Pepsi everywhere in the world except New Zealand, where Pepsi was by far the leader. Then it would be correct to speak of New Zealand as a separate segment, but the rest of the world would be one segment and the marketing scale advantage enjoyed by Coke everywhere else would make New Zealand a barely tenable separate segment for Pepsi. At some point, the most interesting segmentation would have become global, even if national segment enclaves temporarily continued to exist.

Similarly, segments can be carved out or relinquished within a product range. At one time, British motorcycles were the market leaders throughout the world whatever type or power of bike was being considered – motorcycles were one global segment. Then the Japanese began to develop bikes, based around the low-powered vehicles for which there was greatest domestic demand. First, this small engined market became a separate segment in Japan because the market leaders (Honda and Yamaha) were different from the leaders in the rest of the world market (and in Japan in medium and high-performance bikes). Then the Japanese companies, by trial and error, managed to develop a market for their low-power bikes in the US, and then throughout the world, so that small bikes became a separate global segment. Later, using modular designs and high cost-sharing, the Japanese suppliers entered medium-sized bikes and became the market leaders, thus changing the segmentation around the world by annexing the medium market, so that there were two global segments: the low to medium segment (dominated by the Japanese), and the high performance segment, still then dominated by Norton and BSA. Then, in the early 1970s, the Japanese began to edge their way into the high-performance segment, and BMW created a separate high-comfort, high-safety segment, so that the world motorcycle market had two big segments: the 'BMW' segment, and the rest (the majority) of the market, served largely by Japanese competitors.

In diagnosing what segments you are in today – whether the market is one big segment or several small ones – the best way is to set up hypotheses that X market is a separate segment from Y market, and then test according to the following rules. To get the correct answer 95 per cent of the time, ask just two questions:

◆ *Are there separate competitors, with significant market share, in segment X that do not participate in segment Y? If so, it is a separate segment.*

◆ *Are the relative market share positions in market X different from those in market Y, even if the same competitors compete? If so, it is a separate segment.*

For example, Heinz and HP compete in both the ketchup and thick brown sauce markets in the UK, but in the first Heinz is miles ahead of HP, and in the latter HP is way ahead – so they are separate segments.

To be absolutely sure, ask these additional questions:

◆ *Is your firm's profitability different in market X than in market Y? If so, even if it is the same product being supplied to different customers, it may be a separate segment.*

◆ *Are the cost structures different in the two markets?*

◆ *Are there technological barriers between the two markets that only some competitors can surmount?*

◆ *Are prices different (for the same product or service) in the different markets?*

◆ *Is it possible to gain an economic advantage by specializing in one of the markets, by gaining lower costs or higher prices in that market?*

Because segmentation changes over time, it is interesting to look both at the empirical segmentation today, which is defined particularly by the first two questions above, and also at potential segmentation based on the economics of the business: what is called economic segmentation. Economic segmentation applies the second set of questions above to ask not just whether the segmentation is distinct today but whether it could be distinct. Economic segmentation can be used as a technique to resegment a market, either by creating a new, smaller segment out of an existing segment (as with the initial Japanese move to create a low-powered motorcycle segment), or to merge two segments (as with the later annexation of first the mid and then the high performance motorcycle segments) and realize economies of scale. Economic segmentation asks: could we obtain lower costs or higher prices or both by redefining the segment and changing the rules of the game?

STAR

The most exciting of the four positions on the BCG MATRIX. A star is the market leader (has the highest relative market share) in a high growth business (generally over ten per cent a year anticipated volume growth rate in the next three to five years). The star business is immensely valuable if it keeps its leadership position because market growth will make it much bigger and because it should be very profitable, having higher prices or lower costs than lower market share competitors. The star business may not yet be very cash positive, in fact the usual expectation is that it will be broadly cash neutral, since although it earns a lot of profits it will require reinvestment and working capital to continue to grow. But when the market growth slows, if the leadership position has been held, the business will become a large CASH COW and provide a high proportion of cash for the whole business portfolio.

It is said that there are three policy rules for looking after stars: 'invest, invest and invest'. Almost no investment is too great; whatever the financial projections say, any investment is likely to show an excellent return. The worst possible thing to happen to stars is that they lose their leadership position to someone else's QUESTION MARK (which then becomes the new star, relegating the erstwhile star to the position of a question mark and eventually, as growth slows, a DOG). If leadership is lost, the cash previously invested in building up the (former) star may never be recovered, and for all the glamour the business would have proved a cash trap. Hence the necessity to invest to hold the star's leadership position, and if possible extend it, so that competitors can never catch up. This may require very rapid growth, perhaps up to 40–50 per cent a year, which requires skilful management and possibly large amounts of cash.

Star businesses are rare. But star businesses that are well managed and that keep their leadership positions are even rarer. The Model T Ford was once a star but lost its leadership position, became a question mark and eventually a dog. The Xerox range of photocopiers, Kodak cameras, TI (US) semiconductor chips, DuPont synthetic fibers, Gestetner office machine and Hilton hotels are all examples of one-time stars that became dogs, and never yielded the anticipated returns to investors. On the other hand, McDonald's hamburger restaurants, the Sony Walkman, and Coca-Cola are all examples of former stars that held their star status until the market growth slowed, and have since become enormous CASH COWS and given fantastic returns to shareholders. Filofax is an example of a business that lost its STAR position in personal organizers (outside the US), but then recovered it again. It is interesting that in all these cases the stock market fortunes of the companies reflected what BCG said would happen, with a time lag. All of these businesses were highly valued by the stock market when they were STARS, often on PEs of 50 or more. Those businesses that lost share and ended up as DOGS were over-valued and never fulfilled the implied promise; those that held on to leadership amply justified the confidence of investors.

STRATEGIC BUSINESS UNIT (SBU)

A profit center within a company that is organized as an autonomous unit and that corresponds roughly to one particular market. SBUs originated in the 1970s and have proved popular. The story of how they came about is interesting. SBUs began in 1970 when Fred Borch, head of GE in the US, decided to decentralize, abolish or curtail staff functions, and reorganize on the basis of stand-alone SBUs. GE set up the following criteria for an SBU:

◆ *An SBU must have an external, rather than an internal, market; must have a set of external customers.*

◆ *It should have a clear set of external competitors it is trying to beat.*

◆ *It should have control over its own destiny – decide what products to offer, how to obtain suppliers, and whether or not to use shared corporate resources such as R&D.*

◆ *It must be a profit center, with performance measured by its profits.*

The move to SBUs in GE and in Western countries has on the whole been positive. The drawback with an SBU structure is that it does not encourage full use of the common skill base and technology that a corporation may have, although it does not prevent it either. The SBU structure is not well equipped to deal with the challenge of Japanese companies, which not only draw fully on common internal skills derived from and serving a variety of products but also benefit from each other's skills in an interlocking way.

STRONG FOLLOWER

Business that is between 70 per cent and 99 per cent the size of the segment leader. See MARKET CHALLENGER.

VALUE CHAIN

A company's co-ordinated set of activities to satisfy customer needs, starting with relationships with suppliers and procurement, going through production, selling and marketing, and delivery to the customer. Each stage of the chain is linked with the next, and looks forward to the customer's needs, and backwards from the customer too. Each link in the value chain must seek competitive advantage. It must either be lower cost than the corresponding link in competing firms, or add more value by superior quality or differentiated features. The basic idea behind the value chain has been around since the concept of value added and cost structures, but was made explicit by Michael Porter in 1980.

VALUE DISCIPLINES

Term coined by Michael Treacy and Fred Wiersema in their book *The Discipline of Market Leaders*. The concept rests on two basic tenets:

First, that different customers will value one of three broad, distinct value propositions:

1. Best total cost – a great deal, good value for money; *or*

2. Best product – top of the line, the best product or brand; *or*

3. Best solution – a customized product or service, exactly what I need.

Customers will reward companies that deliver such a clear value proposition, and intuitively know they can't expect more than one of the propositions.

Second, to deliver one of the value propositions and outperform competition, companies have to choose a business model that delivers just that one proposition. These 'value disciplines' are:

1. Operational excellence (for best total cost).

2. Product leadership (for best product).

3. Customer intimacy (for best solution).

Across industries, companies that have chosen to excel in one value discipline are similar in terms of their company culture, business processes and management systems.

Companies that do not choose to focus on one proposition and value discipline will find themselves 'stuck in the middle'. Their departments and employees will try to deliver mutually exclusive types of value to customers, and consequently will overstretch their resources and become high cost, yet below-average at delivering any of the customer propositions.

VISION

An inspiring view of what a company could become, a dream about its future shape and success, a picture of a potential future for a firm, a glimpse into its promised land. A vision is the long-term aspiration of a leader for his or her company, that can be described to colleagues and that will urge them on through the desert.

The word vision is often used as a synonym for mission, particularly in non-English speaking countries, where 'mission' is difficult to translate. But the two concepts are different. Mission is why a firm exists, its role in life. Vision is a view of what the firm could become, imagining a desired future. See also MISSION.

Vision may be thought of as reaching a future goal. A good example of a vision that was fulfilled was President Kennedy's preposterous pledge in 1961 of achieving the goal, before the decade was out, of landing a man on the Moon and returning him safely to Earth. An industrial equivalent may be the number 26 in the world league table of drugs companies aiming to reach the top five by the year 2015. Another popular vision is for a regional (say, European) company to become 'truly global', where this is defined as having at least a quarter of sales and profits in each triad of the world (Americas, Asia and Europe). Or for a small company to become larger than its largest competitor. Or for a derided airline to become 'the world's favorite'.

It was Marvin Bower's vision in the 1940s to think that McKinsey, a small, regional US consultancy, could become a huge firm with offices around the world and with a reputation for developing professional management. Likewise, it was Henry Ford's vision in 1909 to 'democratize the automobile'. Steve Jobs' vision at Apple was to change work habits by making computers user-friendly to normal executives. The vision at IKEA was to change the structure of the furniture market, become the first and leading global competitor in an industry previously dominated by separate national leaders. And so on.

WHITNEY ANALYSIS

Analysis of customers put forward in a 1996 *Harvard Business Review* article by John Whitney. It has proven to be very useful to make a distinction between which customers really need taking care of, which customers derive value from the company and those in between. The analysis evaluates customers on three aspects: *strategic importance; size (or significance)*; and *profitability*.

Strategic importance is, as the name suggests, the customer's long-term importance to the business. It assesses how close the customer's product or service is to the heartland of the supplier's business, and the extent to which the firm and the customer can evolve together, building on each other's strengths.

Size or significance is about a customer's current or future revenues. One objective is to distinguish between small and large customers, because small customers tend to take as much time and effort as larger ones. The second objective is to recognize that it is much more problematic to lose one big customer than several small ones.

Finally, there is *profitability*. Most obviously, this is influenced by price, with higher paying customers expected to be more profitable than lower paying ones. But more often than not, some customers who pay the same price as others take inordinate efforts to serve (and hence are much less profitable than others), whereas others are a breeze. This is hence related closely to the EIGHTY/TWENTY RULE and ACTIVITY-BASED COSTING. Whitney analysis thus requires careful cost allocation not just of manufacturing costs, but also of the business overheads.

All customers are scored a 'yes' or a 'no' on each of the criteria, using a strategic checklist for strategic importance, and cut-off values for each of profitability and size. There are no universal cut-off values for profitability and size – these need to be determined by each company.

Next, the customers can be classified in four broad classes A, B, C and D, and tactics developed for each to maximize value (see Illustration II.17). For example, a business may choose to change its service levels between the different classes, allowing much more leeway to A-class customers, than to the D-class.

While a Whitney analysis can be carried out independently from a strategy development exercise, it is better done at the end of that process, because this:

◆ *allows better insight in what is strategic, and*

◆ *makes it clearer what actions to take to improve the customer mix.*

ILLUSTRATION II.17

Customer classification and typical tactics for Whitney analysis

Strategic	Significant	Profitable	Class	Typical tactics
Yes	Yes	Yes	A	Preferential product availability, free access
Yes	No	Yes	A	to additional services, joint product
				development on offer
Yes	Yes	No	B	Preferential product availability, limited or
Yes	No	No	B	paid access to additional services, joint
No	Yes	Yes	B	development under conditions
No	Yes	No	C	Conditional product availability, no access
				to services
No	No	Yes	D	Transfer to distributor, or conditional
No	No	No	D	product availability at cost coverage, with
				no access to services

For example, one company decided to transfer all its worst customers to distributors, as it did not want to deal with small-volume purchases. Another company decided to raise prices to its worst customers, so that they either became slightly profitable customers, or took their unprofitable business elsewhere.

INDEX

Business Segments

F Membership
S Membership

P b f ← starts
          awards
          sponsphi

Job seekers